What We Inherit

A Secret War and a Family's Search for Answers

Jessica Pearce Rotondi

The Unnamed Press
Los Angeles, CA

AN UNNAMED PRESS BOOK

Copyright © 2020 Jessica Pearce Rotondi

www.unnamedpress.com

Unnamed Press, and the colophon, are registered trademarks of Unnamed
Media LLC.

ISBN: 978-1-951213-07-7
eISBN: 978-1-951213-08-4
Library of Congress Control Number: 2019956850

This is a work of creative nonfiction depicting actual events. All persons within
are real individuals. There are no composite characters. Scenes and dialogue
are drawn from extensive primary source materials, personal interviews, and
that favorite tool of memoirists: memory. Given the nature of memory, some
dialogue is not a word-for-word transcription but rather a representation true to
the spirit of what was said. My family searched for Jack for thirty-six years; this
book condenses that search into key moments in the name of narrative flow.

Cover Design by Robert Bieselin
Designed and Typeset by Jaya Nicely
Manufactured in the United States of America by Versa Press, Inc.
Distributed by Publishers Group West

First Edition

For Mom

CHINA

NORTH
VIETNAM

Hanoi

Gulf of
Tonkin

LAOS

Vientiane

Chiang Mai

Mekong River

Savannakhet

Sepon

THAILAND

Bangkok

CAMBODIA

SOUTH
VIETNAM

Phnom
Penh

Gulf of
Thailand

Saigon

HO CHI MINH TRAIL

LAOS IN 1972

Contents

A mighty lesson we inherit:
Thou art a symbol and a sign
    To Mortals of their fate and force;
Like thee, Man is in part divine,
    A troubled stream from a pure source;
And Man in portions can foresee
His own funereal destiny;
His wretchedness, and his resistance,
And his sad unallied existence:
To which his Spirit may oppose
Itself—and equal to all woes,
    And a firm will, and a deep sense,
Which even in torture can descry
    Its own concenter'd recompense,
Triumphant where it dares defy....

—Lord Byron, "Prometheus"

What We Inherit

Prologue

O urs is a family that loses children. Grandpa Ed cheated death when he jumped out of a burning plane at twenty-two. He was thrown out to the Western Front so fast he hadn't been trained to use a parachute. The German farmers who found him in their field sent him to Stalag 17 for two and a half years, a stint that saved his life but marked the man for good; he could never again stomach the smell of soup, though he let his grandkids play with his prison spoon.

It was Ed's brother we lost, long after the war; he drowned while on vacation in a lake, his young son and daughter watching him kick and splash as the canoe drifted away.

Ed's oldest son and namesake, Edwin "Jack" Pearce, followed his father into the Air Force. He disappeared over the mountains of Laos at twenty-four and stayed missing for thirty-six years.

Ed's daughter—my mother—found her tumor in the shower at fifty-three.

The hearts of some families would have drowned with that first boy, stopped with that plane crash, frozen at that moment of discovery; ours kept beating because we knew what it was to wait.

Part 1 / Faith

Operation Homecoming

"On prime-time news they showed men coming off planes and I'd think, *He's probably on this plane, they just didn't know it. He was over there and came back once; he can do it again*," my uncle Kim tells me. He was eighteen years old when Operation Homecoming aired on TV on February 12, 1973. Kim watched from the yellow floral couch in the Pearce family home off Pennsylvania's Route 6, the house his big brother had visited just months earlier between his first and second tours of duty with the Air Force. TV stations across the United States broadcast footage of the forty American boys being released from North Vietnamese prison camps. The soldiers were skinny on those overly bright screens, but smiling. They stumbled toward the big American plane with the red cross on its wing that shimmered like a mirage above the tarmac of Hanoi's Gia Lam Airport. It was as if the dead were walking, the jumpsuits their captors had issued as gray as their skin in the tropical sun. It was a made-for-TV moment: the plane, the boys, and a young soldier in front, Air Force technical sergeant James R. Cook, saluting the American flag as he was carried on a stretcher aboard the C-141A Starlifter jet that would transport him home.

Three other planes loaded down with prisoners of war took off from Hanoi that day, joined by one from Saigon. The men were deposited at Clark Air Base in the Philippines for an official debriefing, followed by steaks and ice cream, a detail that always makes me stop and think of my grandfather's prison spoon. The freed men were met by Admiral Noel Gayler, commander of U.S. forces in the Pacific and former director of the National Security Agency, and Roger Shields, deputy assistant secretary of defense for POW / MIA affairs—men whose signatures I would later read on yellowing pieces of paper addressed to my grandparents.

My youngest uncle continued to stare at the planes on that screen as if unbroken eye contact could summon his big brother through the airwaves: "Our family would watch the news and get quiet, all of us thinking as we watched another man arrive home, *That's a lucky person there, that's a lucky person there,*" he tells me.

By March 1973, 566 American servicemen were returned to the United States, including 513 men previously listed as missing in action, or MIA. Most were not so lucky; at the close of Operation Homecoming, 1,303 Americans were still unaccounted for. As the rest of the country moved on from the Vietnam War and became swept up in the Watergate scandal, a vocal minority continued to hound the government for answers about what happened to the men who never came home.

My grandparents and mother were leaders among them. Their son and brother—my uncle Jack—disappeared on March 29, 1972, during a nighttime mission over the officially neutral . country of Laos, a country the United States dropped more bombs on between 1964 and 1973 than it did on Germany and Japan combined during World War II.

Long, thin Laos, situated between Thailand to the west, China to the north, Vietnam to the east, and Cambodia to the south, was critical to Dwight D. Eisenhower's domino theory of keeping communism at bay: "If Laos were lost, the rest of Southeast Asia would follow," he told his National Security Council. By the early 1960s, Laos was a nation at war with itself. Newly free of its colonial overlords, it was teetering between a conservative military government backed by the United States, a communist one supported by Vietnam and China, and a coalition government attempting to precariously balance the two. On the day of his farewell address as president, Eisenhower approved the C.I.A.'s covert training of anticommunist forces in the mountains of Laos. His successors in the White House—John F. Kennedy, Lyndon B. Johnson, and Richard Nixon—all approved escalating air support for the guerrilla fighters, a decision that would ultimately make Laos the most heavily bombed country per capita in the world.

Of all the prisoners returned in Operation Homecoming, only nine were captured in Laos, and those "lucky" men were all in North Vietnamese custody before their release. For years, the United States claimed that all the men were brought home, though documents declassified as late as 1994 said that the C.I.A. and Defense Intelligence Agency (D.I.A.) knew of up to forty-one Americans left behind in captivity in Laos at war's end. As my father said, "How bad would it have looked if they knew there were men there and didn't get them out?"

By the end of the war in Laos in 1975, two hundred thousand civilians and members of the military were dead. Almost twice as many were wounded, and 750,000 people—nearly a quarter of the population— had become refugees. In comparison, declassified documents show that 728 Americans died in Laos, though most were working for the C.I.A. and not revealed to the U.S. public for decades.

My family's demands for a full accounting of the missing was an uncomfortable reminder of a conflict most Americans would prefer to forget and a shadow war the government refused to acknowledge. I see my uncle Kim staring at that screen in 1973 and draw a direct line to Mom four decades later, undergoing a Hail Mary clinical trial for her stage 4 cancer, when the Air Force calls to tell her "we've found something." My mother was given months to live and lasted three years, long enough to learn what happened to her brother and bring him home.

The Lao believe the spirits of the dead coexist with the living, that they must be appeased with offerings and spoken to aloud. In the months after Mom's death, I looked for signs from her everywhere, bargained for her attention, for her time, for dreams of her that would not come. Traveling to the mountains in Laos where her brother was lost—a place she obsessively circled on maps but never visited—was my way of bringing her back to me, of meeting the woman I never got to know. To find out what happened to Jack was to find out why we don't talk about death in the Pearce family, why we cling to hope past its expiration date. I wanted to know Jack so I could understand her.

To do that, I had to unbury them both.

1 / The Discovery

I'll never give up. If I have to go in myself
and look for him, I'll do it.
—Linda Pearce Rotondi

I am eight years old the first time I hear the name Jack, playing
on the floor of my parents' bedroom, the mahogany of Mom's
monogrammed jewelry box smooth on my lap. I often borrowed
things from it, tried them on for size. A favorite is the opal sliver
of a ring Dad gave her on their honeymoon. The stone chipped
within a week. *It's bad luck to wear opals if they're not your birthstone,*
Mom always said—but it is *my* birthstone, and I love to watch the
red and green flecks catch fire as it warms to my hand. I'd taken to
wearing the ring to school, to play practice, slipping it back into its
familiar place when Mom wasn't looking.

I run my fingers across my favorite seashell-pink cameo ring
that rattles in its setting, property of Great-Aunt Something, and
my hand stops. Dark against the wine-colored velvet is a ring I
have never seen before: a deep garnet stone, square, the silver
setting around it curved like crested waves holding back a pool of
blood. I untangle it from a silver necklace chain and start to slide it
over the knuckle of my ring finger.

"Put that back."

Mom is behind me; I hadn't realized she'd entered the room.

"I've never seen this one before! Is it new?"

"Jessica, put that down."

"Where did you get it?" I can't stop staring at the color; it's the deepest red I've ever seen.

She sighs. "Thailand."

"I didn't know you went to Thailand!"

"I didn't. It was a gift."

"From Dad?" (At eight, your idea of who can give your mother jewelry is fairly limited.)

She takes the ring forcibly from my finger, leaving the skin pink. "My brother Jack." Softening. "A long time ago."

She puts it back in the box and closes it.

"Please don't go through my things."

And I didn't, until she was dead at fifty-six and I was kneeling on the floor of her closet, surrounded by boxes of letters about the brother she never talked about.

West Newbury, Massachusetts • October 29, 2009 • Mom gone 4 hours

Jack came surging back into my life hours after Mom left it. The house felt foreign as Dad's car pulled up, as if I hadn't spent my whole life running beneath the tall pines in the backyard. Their Christmas tree smell was strong even in summer, when rain dripped down the wisteria vines framing the front door and the shape-shifting boxwoods out back, victims of the deer who'd steal out of the trees each night to return Mom's careful pruning to wildness. But it was fall now, the smoke from the neighbors' burning leaf pile edging into the air, cold snaps shrinking the wisteria back toward its roots.

The recessed bulbs in the entryway hum and warm in their sockets as I flick on the switch. The kitchen before me is barely recognizable. Mom's blue-and-white china dishes—gifts from my father to my mother, collected piece by piece over Christmases and anniversaries—are stacked like vertebrae in the sink, slowly fusing with food. The counters are covered in half-crumpled shopping bags from the local pharmacy, drug interaction packets still stapled to empty paper sleeves. *Tamoxifen. Faslodex.* I don't need to check the labels to know the side effects: vision problems, depression, bone pain. A recipe for a sick woman in her own kitchen.

Mom always downplayed the seriousness of it all on the phone: *Oh, it's pill time; I have to hang up, honey. My fingers have been a little sore this week; I couldn't write you a note.* On those days when I called on my lunch break from New York and Dad told me, *Your mother can't talk right now, Jess. She's sleeping,* I always called back. I sent her books by the pile, wanting to fill her with all the words I couldn't manage to say over the phone.

I leave the empty pharmacy bags behind and head to her home office. The brass lamp I switch on reflects off the hunter-green walls, making Mom's desk look like it's underwater. In the last few months, our nightly phone calls from Massachusetts to New York had turned to the screenplay she was writing about cancer. *Something to make other women feel less alone,* she'd said. But whenever I asked her about it, she always put me off: *It's not ready yet. It needs to cook a bit.* The woman wrote thank-you notes for thank-you notes, left detailed marginalia in cookbooks about oven temperature; surely she'd left something behind that would tell her daughters what, exactly, she expected us to do without her.

Mom's laptop is propped open but dark. The power key gives easily as I press down, slicked with the oil from repeated human touch. The keyboard whirs beneath my palm as the screen blinks awake, throwing bluish light over my arms. A daisy avatar pops up on-screen labeled "Linda." I click on it. For once, I'm grateful Mom didn't bother with a password.

The front door opens, and I can hear Dad helping my grandmother into the house, my younger sister behind them. I grow self-conscious about sitting in Mom's chair, of not going to them, but stay where I am.

The screen refreshes, revealing a desktop with exactly two icons: Mail and Internet Explorer. Microsoft Word isn't even installed.

I check the trash. Temporary files. Nothing.

My eyes catch the glow of more brass—the knob to the desk's solitary drawer. I pull it toward me and my breath quickens: there, tucked behind a stack of note cards, is the red leather journal I had bought her a few years back, its red silk bookmark ribbon dangling promisingly about a quarter of the way through. I rip it open and start turning its pages in the computer screen's sterile light, my hands shaking from the cups of hospital coffee, the ups and downs of ambulance rides, and strangers telling me they're so, so sorry. The anger rises up as I flip through it. Only a few of the pages are filled out, mostly fragments of travel notes about where she ate lunch. Mom stopped writing in it long before she got sick.

There's only one other place.

I stare at the hallway stairs for a minute before starting up, forcing myself to grip the oak banister that wobbles and creaks with every step. Dad said that Mom had been unable to come down them for the past week, but I hadn't believed him at the time. *My mother may be sick, but she can walk down a flight of damn stairs.* I reach the top of them now and let myself look back down with the eyes of a frightened woman trapped in her body, no longer able to leave her own home.

I head for the bedroom where my mother spent the last summer of her life and swing open the door. The indent of Mom's head is still pressed into the pillow. A few silver hairs float up like dandelion bracts in the stale air, vibrating with my breath. Books are stacked along the floor on her side of the bed—the contents of all the packages I sent that she will never read.

I step over the books and reach for the closet door. When I flip the switch, the shadows flee from Mom's dresses, their emptiness more pronounced in the harsh light. I run my hands over her things, the sheets of thin dry cleaner's plastic clinging to my arms like I clung to hers as I leaned over her hospice bed only hours earlier.

I reach for Mom's red coat at the back of the closet and my hand bumps up against something hard. Pulling aside her silk blouses and creased wool pants, I uncover an old filing cabinet shoved against the wall.

The shelves rock but don't budge when I pull at the handle of the cabinet's top drawer. I tug harder, knuckles whitening, knocking her coat to the floor. When the drawer finally jerks open, it's easy to see why it had been stuck shut: it is filled to bursting with newspaper clippings. I pull out a stack and see my grandparents' faces over and over, headlines screaming for their son:

STALAG 17 SURVIVOR WAGES 10-YEAR BATTLE TO LEARN FATE OF MIA SON

FAMILIES WORK WITH BELIEF THAT MIAS ARE ALIVE IN ASIA

MILFORD MAN GOES TO LAOS IN SEARCH OF MISSING SON

MIA FATHER KEEPS THE FAITH

TROOPER PRESSES MISSION TO FIND SON LOST IN 1972 COMBAT IN LAOS

There are quotes from Mom in these pages, photos of her holding signs about her missing brother as she marches on Washington. How had I never seen these before? My fingers shake as I put the newspaper clippings aside and reach into the drawer again, pulling up a thick scrapbook. Inside, its pages are filled with headshots of young men with stiff Air Force hats clamped to their heads, their newly buzzed hair just visible above formal collars. Some gaze at the camera confidently, their broad shoulders filling the frame, while others appear too young for the uniforms buttoned around their necks. Under every face is the exhortation "WHERE IS HE?"

My uncle Jack's face is on page three.

I have seen only two photos of Jack in my entire life and know exactly that number of things about him: that he was named after his father and that, like his father, he joined the Air Force and was shot down. The only difference was that Jack never came home.

Page after page of heavily censored documents bear my uncle's name. I spread them out across the floor, shoving Mom's shoes aside in the process. The pages are covered in C.I.A. stamps and tantalizing black bars as thick as the silence between Mom and me when it came to her missing brother.

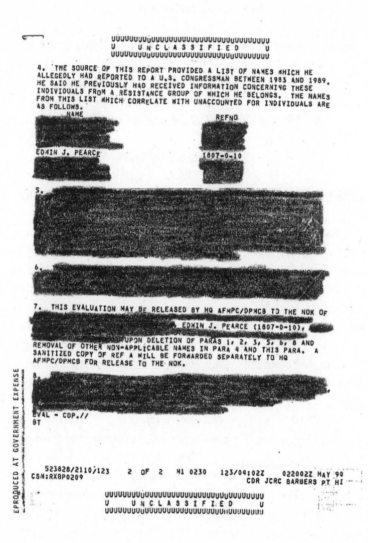

UUUUUUUUUUUUUUUUUUUUUUUUUUUUUUUUUUUU
U   U N C L A S S I F I E D   U
UUUUUUUUUUUUUUUUUUUUUUUUUUUUUUUUUUUU

4. THE SOURCE OF THIS REPORT PROVIDED A LIST OF NAMES WHICH HE
ALLEGEDLY HAD REPORTED TO A U.S. CONGRESSMAN BETWEEN 1983 AND 1989.
HE SAID HE PREVIOUSLY HAD RECEIVED INFORMATION CONCERNING THESE
INDIVIDUALS FROM A RESISTANCE GROUP OF WHICH HE BELONGS. THE NAMES
FROM THIS LIST WHICH CORRELATE WITH UNACCOUNTED FOR INDIVIDUALS ARE
AS FOLLOWS.

NAME   REFNO

EDWIN J. PEARCE   1807-0-10

5.

6.

7. THIS EVALUATION MAY BE RELEASED BY HQ AFMPC/DPMCB TO THE NOK OF
                         EDWIN J. PEARCE (1807-0-10),
                    UPON DELETION OF PARAS 1, 2, 3, 5, 6, 8 AND
REMOVAL OF OTHER NON-APPLICABLE NAMES IN PARA 4 AND THIS PARA. A
SANITIZED COPY OF REF A WILL BE FORWARDED SEPARATELY TO HQ
AFMPC/DPMCB FOR RELEASE TO THE NOK.

8.

EVAL - COP.//
BT

523828/2110/123   2 OF 2   MI 0230   123/04:02Z   022002Z MAY 90
CSN:RX8P0209   CDR JCRC BARBERS PT HI

UUUUUUUUUUUUUUUUUUUUUUUUUUUUUUUUUUUU
U   U N C L A S S I F I E D   U
UUUUUUUUUUUUUUUUUUUUUUUUUUUUUUUUUUUU

The closest I thought I'd been to the C.I.A. was watching spy movies on TV; I never dreamed that there was a stash of declassified files hidden in my childhood home. But it's the next piece of paper that challenges everything I thought I knew about the woman who raised me:

30 April 1977

President Carter
White House
1600 Pennsylvania Avenue NW
Washington, DC 20500

Dear President Carter:

I am writing to you about a very serious personal matter, which you have the power to alter, if you so desire. Since March 29, 1972, I have worked to discover what has happened to my brother, Jack Pearce. It was on that date that the AC-130 he was flying in was shot down over Laos. Besides the fact that one cannot give up hope where a loved one is concerned, *I have reason to believe that my brother may still be alive through concrete evidence.* The accompanying planes heard beeper signals coming from the ground immediately following the crash. This serves to prove that someone survived the crash. Unfortunately, it has been impossible to access the crash site since that date, so further information has not been garnered....

I decided to take matters into my own hands. I traveled to Paris to speak to officials both at the Vietnamese and Laotian embassies concerning my brother's fate. I was politely received at the Vietnamese embassy by Do Thanh, the First Secretary, but I did not gain any satisfactory information. Rather, I was referred to the Laotian embassy due to the location of my brother's crash.

It was at the Laotian Embassy, while speaking to Phanthong Phommahaxay, the Chargé d'Affaires, that I learned some disturbing information.

Phanthong Phommahaxay stressed that no MIA Information will be released to the United States until our country sincerely proved to be friendly. I countered with the fact that the MIA commission's recent trip to Vientiane should prove our country's willingness to establish friendly relations. It was then that I was told that while overtly we attempt to establish friendly relations with the new Lao government, our C.I.A. is undermining it with violent covert activities originating from Thailand. If this is the case, any hope for Americans being held in Laos being humanely released is considerably lessened, if not completely destroyed... this hypercritical action only serves to annihilate American credibility in the diplomatic arena. I would like to urge to you to suspend all such activities if they do, in fact, take place.

Thank you for your consideration in this matter.

Sincerely,
Linda Pearce

I had no idea my mother went to Paris at twenty-two to meet with ambassadors or that she wrote to presidents. The correspondence in front of me continues into the 1990s, the years she was tacking my childish artwork up on the wall and changing my sister's diapers.

I kneel in my dead mother's closet, surrounded by letters about the brother she never talked about and questions the living can't answer.

2 / *Gunner's Moon*

The war will soon be over for most Americans,
but Sergeant Jack Pearce... leaves Ubon, Thailand, for a flight
over Laos. There is a full moon—a gunner's moon, they call it—and it
makes Jack's crew a little uneasy because it gives gunners on the
ground a better shot at a low-flying gunship like the AC-130.
—*Wanted! Dead or Alive: An MIA Documentary*

*M*om was the one tasked with waking her father up for work as a kid. She used to tell me how she'd lightly touch his shoulder and whisper as loud as she dared, *Dad, it's time to get up.*

He used to bolt right up, she'd tell me. For those first few moments, her dad was replaced with another man, his blue eyes seeing soldiers and walls that weren't there. *But then his eyes would find mine*, she'd say, *and he'd come back to me.*

She'd watch him drink his black coffee and eat his cornflakes at the breakfast table before handing him his Pennsylvania state trooper's hat and hugging him goodbye.

He always seemed so big to me, she said. *Like nothing bad could happen to you while he was there.*

Milford, Pennsylvania • March 29, 1972

There is a full moon the night Jack's plane is shot down. A gunner's moon, bright enough to make anything that crosses the clouds an easy target. Grandpa Ed hasn't flown in a waist gunner's seat in years, but the memory of that exposure never leaves you. The waist gunner's view on a B-17 is open to the sky, the cold biting at your face as you cling to the .50-calibers, standing as your captain brings you in low, the houses and roads coming up at you fast in the moonlight.

Ed lies awake next to his wife as the full moon rises over Milford, Pennsylvania, and shines through the white lace curtains Rosemary had sewn in '47, back when she was a new bride and the lawn was dirt and he started having nightmares about the war.

It's often a truck backfiring on Route 6 that sets my grandfather's heart racing, the big ones that lumber down the valley to refuel, passing the small white house in the darkness on their way to northern cities. Sometimes it's the lone cars that wake him, whirring like blood rushing through his ears as they approach. He'll startle awake and hold his breath, following the sound of their engines growing louder until their headlights illuminate the bedroom. There, to his immediate relief, is his wife asleep beside him, lying on her back with her mouth slightly open. His polished boots are lined up against his side of the bed, just as he left them; his kids are smiling up from the mismatched frames on Rosie's dressing table, four boys and a girl holding fishing poles they've long since outgrown. Gone are the prison camp and the cold and the gunfire.

Ed's B-17 was one of 351 Allied planes sent to bomb Schweinfurt, Germany, on October 14, 1943. The heavily defended city was home to multiple ball bearing factories supplying Nazi troops. Ed's plane was nicknamed "Patches" for the number of repairs it had undergone, an appearance that belied the valuable cargo it carried: the bombsight that would direct all the other Allied planes where to drop their payload. Only the first three bombers that morning had one on board. It was the equivalent of holding the flag as you charged the front lines.

"Most of the anti-aircraft fire was concentrated upon our plane," my grandfather wrote forty-five years to the day of being shot down. The Germans quickly hit their mark: "We sustained three direct hits from AA shells, knocking out most of our power, and including a large hole in No. 2 wing tank. We managed to drop our bombs on the target even though we had a severe gasoline leak."

My grandfather watched the bombs fall thousands of feet below, along with the gasoline streaming rapidly from his plane.

> As we turned back toward France after leaving the target we were swarmed by enemy fighters. We soon caught fire and the order was given to bail out. We were over 23,000 ft. alt. at this time. None of us had ever received parachute training and we did not have our parachute harnesses on tight enough...

Ed had been rushed out to the war at nineteen, deployed so quickly that there hadn't been time to teach him what he was now being ordered to do. His hands shook as he tried to fasten the buckles before diving toward the earth, the smoke from burning gasoline stinging his eyes.

> On the parachute decent [sic], many enemy fighters spilled the air out of our parachutes, causing them to collapse and when they reopened with a snap, this caused additional injury to the already injured groin and back.
> This happened to me five times during the descent.
> A swarm of enemy fighters circled the descending parachutes, spilling the air out and causing the parachutes to be blown away from the wooded area toward the cleared farmland to the North.

The Germans herded them like sheep in the sky, and all Grandpa Ed could do was watch as hundreds of white spots clotted the sun: "I was looking up at the chute instead of the ground when I hit [due to lack of training] and was injured again."

He dislocated his jaw when he fell, his mouth stuck open in awe at the death all around him. Sixty-three other U.S. planes were shot down that day, though the Germans fared worse: 182 of 184 German fighters were shot down in one of the largest air raids in history.

My grandfather came to in a German field. Much to his relief, the farmers who found him didn't shoot him but rounded him up to be interrogated. The captured men were loaded into boxcars. Sixty soldiers were crushed into a single car meant for forty. There were no bathrooms, just buckets. They spent that first night in the railroad yards of Frankfurt while Britain's Royal Air Force bombed the city all around them, the loudness of the bombs their only indication of how close they were to being destroyed themselves.

On the second day—it must have been day, because of the cracks of light the men pressed up against the walls of the boxcar could see—the car began to move, the rails screeching beneath them. The men were locked in the hot boxcar for four days. When the train doors opened again, Grandpa Ed found himself behind barbed wire in Krems, Austria.

In his prison ID photo, my grandfather's dark hair is tousled and parted to the right, bangs sweeping across his forehead. Beneath his wild hair, his light eyes stare directly at the camera like the eyes of dead men in Civil War battleground photos. He'd later tell us that he had tried to cover his face as much as possible in case he had the chance to escape.

Ed Pearce's prisoner of war identification card from Stalag 17.

He spent the next two winters in the unheated barracks of Stalag 17-B, the prison that would later be the namesake for the 1953 movie directed by Billy Wilder. Ed's daily ration of food was a small portion of watery soup from a large wooden tub ("one hundred fifty men to a tub," my grandfather notes indignantly) and "a small piece of black bread."

Each prisoner was given an aluminum spoon. At the time, my grandfather thought that if he ever got out, he'd never want to see that damn spoon again. But once the camp was liberated, he found he couldn't leave the thing behind. It was a reminder of all the sorry meals he'd eaten with it that kept him alive.

> In the nineteen plus months we spent there I can remember only three hot showers... The barracks themselves were built over a crawl space and during the winter, snow would blow under and come up between the cracks in the floor. Those of us who lost our boots bailing out were particularly exposed to frostbitten feet.

Even as an old man, my grandfather's feet bothered him. They'd tingle and then lose feeling. Like his daughter during chemo decades later, he never felt truly warm.

When the Russians advanced to Vienna in March 1945, my grandfather marched with five hundred other POWs across the Austrian Alps: "We slept on the ground in the rain or snow and our ration of food was one small portion of soup a day. There was not always enough to go around and some of us went for two or three days with nothing to eat."

I think of my grandmother's kitchen, always so full of food, the second helpings she heaped on my grandfather at every turn. He returned from war severely underweight for his six-foot frame, and even in old age, he had the lean legs of a marathoner.

My grandfather was liberated by General George S. Patton's Thirteenth Tank Corps, Third Army, on May 10, 1945. From Austria, he was flown to France, where he was able to send a telegram to his mother—his first contact with her in over six months. When I find the letter in my mother's papers, it is encased in plastic like a slide specimen:

May 12, 1945

Dear Mom,
Will be home as soon as possible—expect to be there shortly. Tell everyone I was asking for them. Hope everything is OK. I am well. I haven't heard from you since Nov. 2, 1944. So you can see I have as many questions to ask that I don't know where to begin so I'll wait till I get home.

Loads of Love,
Eddie

I imagine my grandfather counting all 191 days of silence between them, turning over his curious phrasing in my mind: *So you can see I have as many questions to ask that I don't know where to begin.* I wonder if he and his mother ever did begin to talk about what happened during the war. What it was like for my great-grandmother to wait for news while going about her daily life, what it was like for Ed to wake up and go to sleep in the same dreary barracks, unsure if he'd ever see home again. In his telegram, where every letter counts, he used the word "home" twice.

Grandpa Ed was honorably discharged from the Military on September 26, 1945. In March 1946, he was approved for a disability pension, the reason listed simply as "nervous condition 50%." His firstborn son and namesake, Edwin Jack Pearce, was born on December 8 the following year.

Jack followed his father into the Air Force, the stories of the B-17s Ed flew over Germany pulling at the boy's imagination, bleeding into history projects at school where Ed would talk about what he did during the war to classrooms full of kids who just wanted to know if he'd ever killed anybody. By the time Jack was old enough to join up, America was embroiled in Vietnam.

As Ed lies in bed in Milford, his son is on his second tour of duty flying nighttime missions out of Thailand. Ed had told his son that he was proud of him—he'd made sure to tell him that.

Under the bright full moon, my grandfather feels that old tightness in the pit of his stomach until the sun slips under the curtains and across the floor. By the time he gets up, his youngest son, Kim, just sixteen, is already in his first class down the street at Delaware Valley High School. Mom is a freshman at Mansfield State College, her older brothers scattered to their various posts: Mike with the Navy in Italy, Bob with the Marines in Japan, and Jack with the Air Force in Thailand.

Ed has to walk by the framed portraits of Jack and my mother hanging in the hallway to enter the blue-and-white-wallpapered kitchen. I picture him there in his cotton undershirt, thick brows wild above eyes the color of a cloudless sky, and want to stop the clock, make it like any other morning; to stand with him as he rinses the remnants of yesterday's coffee from the percolator before flicking on the gas stove with his wrist. It always takes a few clicks before the stench of sulfur flares up, hot and pungent, to his unshaven face. My grandmother often joked it was the cups and cups of black coffee Ed drank each morning that put the white hair on his chest, arms, and back. He isn't a smoking man or a drinking man; coffee is the one vice Ed allows himself to relish. That and the pies my grandmother is always "throwing together" for him. With the children moving on, taking off to start their own lives, it must have felt like it did when he and Rosie were just starting out together.

With his focus on the egg timer counting down the seconds until his coffee is ready, it would have been easy to miss the approaching car slow and turn into the tiny driveway, the engine cutting as it parked. I wonder if my grandfather caught the slamming of the two doors or saw the two men approach from the window above the kitchen sink.

Too early for visitors.

I see my grandfather pausing, empty coffee cup in hand. Hear the doorbell ring with its short, high buzz thrumming through the house like a live current

When you send away someone you love, you fantasize about the front door. You sense their familiar shoulders fill its frame when your back is turned; every creak of the screen sticks in your throat. You lie in bed not wondering if you locked up the house but willing someone you're not sure you'll recognize to enter it.

Ed had been the ghost to walk through the front door in '45. Now, he is the parent reaching for the handle.

3 / Drifting

Mothers and wives have been criticized for years for not letting go.
But it wasn't a case of not letting go. We absolutely know
there are men alive and being held in Southeast Asia.
—**Rosemary Pearce**

Chiang Mai, Thailand • November 16, 2013 • Mom gone 4 years, 18 days

"*L*ook! There's one!" Liz shouts.

I look up at the night sky we descended from hours earlier and see a glowing white orb shiver around a tree. The paper lantern hovers, vibrating in the night air, then catches on a tall branch. The crowd gasps, breaks into a million chattering languages. The paper lantern wavers—left, right—then unhooks itself, rising again toward the roundness of the moon.

Every year, followers of the Buddha in Chiang Mai gather under the full moon on the second month in the Lanna calendar to celebrate Yi Peng. The faithful make merit by releasing lanterns into the sky and water. Depending on whom you ask, the act of release means letting go of your troubles or the granting of a wish you send off into the universe.

I could really use the universe's help. My sister, Morgan, retreated to Germany after Mom's death. It's the place she had studied abroad at Mom's insistence—*Go, go, I'll be here when you get back*. She sends letters on my birthday and on holidays describing walks along the Elbe, of dreaming in other languages. Alone in the house in Massachusetts, my father obsessively checks his online dating profiles and forgets to call, all of us left grieving in our own way.

The sensible part of me knew my scattered family wouldn't be waiting for me on the other side of the world, but I was hoping they'd feel closer here than they do in everyday life. When you live away from home when a parent dies, you're able to picture them still there, moving within the walls of the house you grew up in. It's only when you come home that you realize the fantasy you had of them reading in the next room or asleep upstairs is just that: a fantasy. One that disappears as soon as you stand over a trash bag overflowing with their clothing or a pair of their slippers with the toes pressed in, their warmth long gone.

My bedroom back home in Brooklyn has become a museum to Mom's letters. I moved them by the suitcase-full. Photographed and digitized, they bloom with bright sticky notes where a passage has sent me to the library for background research or to the White Pages to contact veterans who served with Jack.

I found thirteen declassified reports about Jack's dog tags and alleged whereabouts. The last report is dated as late as 1986, sent as my mother was teaching me to sit up on my own. But what really got my attention was Grandpa Ed's account of a trip he took in 1973, when he used the family savings to fly across the world in search of his son.

This morning, I landed in Bangkok, where my grandfather's plane touched down forty years ago. I've cashed in every U.S. Savings Bond from every birthday and good report card that Grandpa Ed ever gave me to buy the plane tickets. Tonight, Liz and I are in Chiang Mai for this festival of letting go. Later this week, we'll head to Laos. There, I'll be meeting an interpreter and guide and traveling to the last known place Jack was seen alive: Sepon, also called Xépôn or Tchepone. The Lao village, with its multiple English spellings, had many incarnations in my mother's papers, appearing in black ink on C.I.A. reports and scratched onto legal pads, a dot circled on maps in thick red pen. I'd found it on battle maps in books with arrows pointing to it in angry swirls, indicating skirmishes along the neighboring Ho Chi Minh Trail. It is the village my uncle Jack was bombing the night he disappeared.

Going to Sepon won't change the fact that Mom is gone. It won't bring back Jack or my grandfather, either. But I feel closer to them when I lose myself in their papers. The years slide away, and suddenly Mom's loss is my loss, her maps a guide to grieving she never meant to leave me.

"Jess, are you okay?"

My eyes leave the sky and move toward my friend Liz's voice. Her pink face is streaked with concern, her thick eyebrows twisted in a *what is going on?* expression. She has sworn off makeup for the trip, the only thing between her perfect Minnesotan pores and the night air a small, white streak of sunscreen dried by her left ear.

"I'm fine."

My head feels as huge as the lanterns bobbing above our heads. The stuffiness pressing in on my skull on my last night in Brooklyn has turned into a full-blown cold. The fever coursing through me makes the edges of the rising lanterns blur, leaving trails like comets in their wake.

I try to smile, but Liz doesn't look convinced. I reach for her and give her arm a squeeze. "I was just thinking how lucky I am that you came with me. You hardly ever get time off; you should have used it to go somewhere with Dave."

One short year ago, I stood next to Liz in an eggplant-purple dress as she married our friend Dave. I've known them both since day one of college. My very first memory of Liz is a firm, friendly handshake, followed by watching her solve a Rubik's Cube in less than five minutes for a room filled with wowed freshmen. Sweet smile, scary smarts—exactly the travel partner you want to accompany you around the world. I was shocked when she'd said yes to coming on the trip. With my sister starting over in Germany and Dad dating in Boston, I had turned to a small group of college friends to ask if anyone wanted to join me. Liz was a newlywed busy applying to business school, but she'd stared me straight in the eye and told me, *I loved your mom. And if you think I'm letting you do this alone, you're insane.*

Liz looks at me now in the dark field in Chiang Mai: "Where would I go that would be as exciting as Thailand and Laos with you?" she asks.

"Someplace in the Bahamas with one of those pool bars you swim up to and rose petals on the bed?"

Liz laughs.

We pass a stopped car, its trunk overflowing with lanterns.

"One hundred baht, one hundred baht for American girls."

Liz's blue eyes sparkle in the headlights as she turns to face me, one eyebrow raised. "Do we really look that American?"

I take in our matching dirty-blond hair, T-shirts, and jeans. "Well, the price is right," I offer.

I hand over a rust-colored note to the spot-on salesman and get a flat circle of white paper and wire in return. The paper sticks to my sweaty arms in the heat.

"Let's light this thing," Liz says, and grins.

She pulls me forward through air thick with burning wicks. All around us, people hold folded white lanterns over their heads as they climb the hill to avoid pulls and tears from the press of bodies. I follow their lead and lift our single lantern against my forehead.

Sweat drips down the space between my shoulder blades as we fight against the current of foot traffic, aiming for a thin row of trees just off the main path. When we get there, finally free of the jostling throng, we lean against the smooth trunks, gulping down air. I pray to whatever god is listening, *Please don't let me pass out.*

Beneath us, the earth buckles and rises in a giant clearing studded with thousands of iron torches, each one topped with a flickering candle. From this height, it looks like a giant birthday cake.

I look from the field of torches to Liz, her face half shadow and half jumping orange flame. I am surrounded by warm night air, a foreign language, and I am a million miles away from home. And right now, that is exactly where I want to be.

Mom was the editor of a prominent medical journal before she gave it all up to have kids. I've spent the past four years working my way up from an assistant at a nonprofit to a senior editor at a major news outlet. This job feels like the closest I can get to giving her the alternate life that being our mother had taken from her. I spend ten-hour workdays submerged in editing pieces by women about everything from dating advice for twentysomethings to parenting and aging to tips on Alzheimer's caregiving. My special area of coverage is breast cancer. I edit story after story about women losing their mothers, about sisters getting sick. I digitally crop photos of women in soft hats with sunken faces, stopping myself just short of imagining Mom's.

On good days, these women feel like family. I work with them on their stories of IVF and childbirth and rediscovering their spouses once their kids move away. It's a chorus of women's voices I want so badly in my life, a guide to the progression of things. It's only when I stop working that I realize the stories are not mine; that, cut off from my mother, I feel unnatural and strange, stuck in my small apartment and unable to advance in anything but work. I want to rejoin the world of the living, reclaim my bedroom from the boxes. But first I need to learn to let go.

"Ready?" Liz asks.

I tuck my hair behind my ears and follow her into the valley of light. The air down here is even warmer, humming with voices and crackling flame. In the crowd's center is a giant seated figure—a Buddha statue several stories tall. The Buddha's face is illuminated from below by the hot light of hundreds of candles set on steps leading to his crossed legs. Above him is the full moon, crowned by a circle of clouds tinged with lantern smoke.

The sound of chanting rises all around us. Liz and I stand as the incantation swells. A single voice comes over the microphone and asks us to fill our hearts and minds with loving-kindness to create room for the merit we are about to make.

Thousands of once-folded lanterns are snapped open against the night sky, and for a moment, I can see Mom standing over my childhood bed, her hands on freshly pressed sheets. She would count to three before lifting the top sheet high in the air, letting it rise up before it drifted down over me like a parachute. I'd lose her face for a minute before the warm fabric fell to the bed and she appeared again, tucking me in safe at the edges.

I look down at my own arms, holding one side of our lantern down over the sputtering flame glowing blue, now red. As the *khom loi* fills with hot air, it tugs at our hands, near to bursting.

White mounds ripple in every direction as couples and siblings and strangers release their lanterns into the sky. Ours lifts with them, and the lamps pulse like jellyfish, weightless, circling one another as they rise. I stare until ours becomes indistinguishable from the other white flecks draining toward the pull of the moon.

Yi Peng lantern release in Chiang Mai, Thailand, November 16, 2013.

4 / *Lost*

I thought it was the end when my plane was shot down on
Oct. 14, 1943 and I was a POW until May, 1945. But I did come
out of it, got married and had children... I have the underlying hope
that Jack will have the same experience I did in World War II.
—Ed Pearce

Vientiane, Laos • October 13, 1973 • Jack missing 1 year, 6 months, 14 days

*M*y grandfather arrives in the Lao capital of Vientiane on
October 13, 1973, forty years before I do. He is fifty-one
years old, his dark blond hair just starting to silver. All around
him, vendors line the streets selling fried plantains and glistening
meat on spits, while children dart through the grown-ups to splash
each other with water from buckets. The city is celebrating Boun
Ok Phansa, the end of Buddhist Lent, when monks are welcomed
back from their rainy season retreat in the mountains.

There is a lot more to celebrate this year. The Paris Peace
Accords ending U.S. involvement in Vietnam were signed in
January, and on September 14, a cease-fire was signed between
the Pathet Lao, aligned with the North Vietnamese government,
and the Royal Lao, the faction covertly supported by the C.I.A.
Between 1964 and 1973, the United States dropped two and a half
million tons of bombs over Laos, or a planeload of bombs every
eight minutes, twenty-four hours a day, for nine years—a rainy
season seemingly without end.

For most Americans, the signing of the peace treaty signaled
a closed chapter, an end to the draft taking their sons and to the
horror stories on the evening news. Not for Ed.

My grandfather had opened the front door a little after nine A.M. on March 29, 1972, to find his local pastor and a total stranger in full Air Force uniform standing on his doorstep, an envelope in his gloved hand. Ed had known the stranger's rank immediately from the gold oak leaf pinned to his chest. Ed had invited the Air Force major and Reverend Edwards into the kitchen and served them fresh coffee.

When he'd gone to wake Rosemary, she hadn't bothered with stockings. Ed had found himself following her, still buttoning the shirt she'd thrown at him, as she stormed into the kitchen. I imagine her taking in the minister's collar, the Air Force uniform. Ed must have seen the look in my grandmother's eyes, the one that everyone in the family knew meant business: *You are in my home, and I need you to tell me what happened to my son.*

My grandparents had stood side by side as Major Howard pulled a piece of paper out of the envelope he'd been carrying. For a moment, the kitchen lamp had illuminated the Air Force seal through the thin sheet, the eagle's outline appearing in reverse. Ed had pulled back a chair just as my grandmother fell into it.

> It is with sincere regret and deep personal concern that I inform you of the circumstances under which your son, Staff Sergeant Edwin Jack Pearce, was declared missing in action.
>
> Jack was a gunner on an AC-130 Gunship in an armed reconnaissance mission over a heavily defended hostile area in Laos on March 29, 1972. At approximately 3:00 A.M., the escort aircraft observed a surface-to-air missile detonation near your son's aircraft. A few seconds later, another surface-to-air missile apparently hit the gunship. The escort flew over the area of the wreckage several times and observed a fire but there was no sign of survivors. However, as they were departing the area about ten minutes later, a survival radio beeper transmission

was received from the direction of the crash site. Other aircraft in the area also heard the transmission; however, no voice contact was ever established. Search and rescue efforts were initiated immediately and electronic surveillance has been continuous, but with negative results other than the original survival radio beacon signals. Electronic surveillance is still in progress.

A detailed report is being compiled at this time concerning the incident. You will be advised by the Casualty Division, USA Military Personnel Center, Randolph Air Force Base, Texas, as to any further information upon completion of the report.

Your son's dedication to duty, professionalism and bravery are in the highest traditions of the United States Air Force. On behalf of Jack's many friends in the 16th Special Operations Squadron and the 8th Tactical Fighter Wing, please accept my deepest personal sympathy at this time of anxiety.

Sincerely,
Carl S. Miller, Colonel
USAF Commander

Fire. No sign of survivors. Pilots in the air above, hearing SOS signals rising from the wreckage in spite of the flames. My grandfather will fixate on this last reason for hope for years to come. In dreams, he'll find himself beside his son on the jungle floor, radioing for help, the fire all around them, while the escort plane turns away above their heads in the moonlight, always returning too late.

When I revisit my grandfather's trip to Laos forty years later, it's not his bravery in flying across the world to a war zone that impresses me. It's the trip he made the morning he learned his son was shot down.

An hour after the Air Force's visit, my grandfather dropped my grandmother off at the Grand Union to spend the day bagging groceries as her son's plane burned half a world away. Grandpa Ed then reported for duty as a Pennsylvania state trooper, driving his patrol car up Route 6 where it winds into the Poconos. As he drove, the trunks of the fir trees on either side of the two-lane grew blurry. Unable to see the road, he backed the car into a grove of trees and killed the engine.

When he raised his hands to his face to adjust his glasses, he shocked himself by finding tears there, as strange to him as if there had been blood.

Years later, my mother will sit in the driveway of our home in her silver Saab with the keys in the ignition, listening to Eva Cassidy songs on repeat before coming inside. I'll watch her from the front room, never daring to disturb her. She was undergoing a new round of radiation treatment and never let herself cry in the house.

I wish I had been brave enough to open the passenger door and crawl in beside her, let her know she wasn't alone. I wish I could reach through the decades and comfort my grandfather as the woods pressed in around him. That's the thing about learning how to be strong from the people you love; it requires a level of loneliness that's hard to unlearn.

My grandfather left my grandmother home alone to come to Laos. He and Rosemary had agreed they could afford only one ticket, so he booked the $1,000 flight from the States to Southeast Asia on his own, the culmination of months of setting aside part of his state trooper's pay. Rosemary contributed from her Grand Union wages, coming home with paper cuts from the brown paper grocery bags that made him want to kiss her pink hands. Ed would write to her every day, faithfully trekking from temple to temple, buying up postcards already starting to curl in the heat.

Ed is traveling as part of a delegation of fifty-three family members of the missing: twenty-nine parents, fourteen wives, five siblings, and five children, though the State Department had tried to limit the group to just six. The government had warned them that the country was "primitive," that there were no hotels, and that locals were unfriendly in an effort to dissuade them from making the journey. They were cautioned to avoid speaking with the press or pressing the issue of prisoners with the joint government. Many had even been discouraged from speaking to one another about the circumstances of their loss.

But the families were not intimidated so easily. They were all part of the National League of POW/MIA Families, an organization founded in 1970 with the mission of drawing attention to the men left behind in Southeast Asia. Before leaving, the group had wired news of their arrival to Lao diplomats and government officials and planned multiple press conferences in defiance of the government's "helpful suggestions." The September 14 peace agreement between the Royal Lao and Pathet Lao stipulated the full disclosure of the lists of the dead, the captured, and those who died in captivity in Laos would be released thirty days after its signing on October 14, 1973. The families' visit was timed around that date.

The delegation left Los Angeles on October 8 for Honolulu, Hawaii, then stopped over in Guam and Hong Kong to refuel before landing in Bangkok. There, Ed's group was hosted by U.S. ambassador to Thailand Leonard Unger and briefed by Admiral Noel Gayler, commander of U.S. forces in the Pacific— the same man who had greeted freed prisoners during Operation Homecoming that February.

The following day, they met with Brigadier General Robert Kingston, commander of the newly formed Joint Casualty Resolution Center. The JCRC was dedicated to carrying out searches, excavations, and recovery of the remains of missing soldiers. My grandfather flew to the JCRC's headquarters at Nakhon Phanom Royal Thai Air Force Base with another MIA father, George Brooks. The two men were shocked to realize the facility often had less information on the details of loss incidents than they had access to simply by banding together with other families. In two cases, they discovered that the missing soldiers they asked about were classified as prisoners of war by the JCRC when their families had only been told that they were missing in action. "I am not a criticizer of the government," Brooks told his local newspaper, "but there are people in the government who are not doing their job."

Kingston promised the two fathers that he would contact Washington about the discrepancies, but my grandfather's trust in him never recovered. Many of the crash sites Kingston was tasked with exhuming were still inaccessible to him and his men, the terrain controlled by communist forces unwilling to invite Americans to dig up the past.

"Time in Laos has very little meaning," Kingston told my grandfather.

The Lao are concerned with things other than lists of prisoners at the moment—like neutralizing the capital city with Pathet Lao police and the formation of a new joint government. The coalition government has been in power only since September, and everywhere Ed looks, men in uniform monitor the crowd. To Ed, it seems that officers the world over are the same: chest forward, a certain vigilance visible in their necks as they walk among men. I imagine him trying to see the city's residents like they do—troublemaker, family, friend—but with the sun in his eyes and new smells all around him, he must have been unmoored, drifting in a sea of people who do not know him or why he is here. His uniform and badge are packed away at home, the short-sleeved collared shirt sticking to his back making him just another American unaccustomed to the heat, perhaps attached to the military, perhaps just passing through.

A cheer swells up from the crowd as a race finishes up on the water. In the middle of it, a wail makes Ed start. He turns in the direction of the sound and sees a boy no older than five standing by one of the police officers, sobbing uncontrollably. As my grandfather approaches, the small boy's sobs turn to whimpers as he takes in the American stranger.

The officer startles Ed by explaining in English that the child is lost. Custom, he says, dictates that the police hold him until he finds his family. Nearly four decades after this encounter, I read the newspaper account detailing this meeting between the American ex-POW searching for his son and the missing Lao child and can't think of a better way to sum up the tragedy of the whole damn war.

My grandfather reaches into his pocket and pulls out a sleeve of Life Savers candies he's brought from home and hands one to the boy. Ed watches him take it as if it's the Host at Communion. The sound of young women laughing makes my grandfather turn. Two slim women in their twenties approach, nodding at Ed in appreciation for what he's done for the child. The one in front extends a pale forearm to hold her parasol over his thinning hair. The light around him is dappled, the Mekong bouncing sunlight onto their faces. Maybe it's the lost boy, the laughing women, or the sun warming his head, but whatever it is, Ed tells the papers back home that if the people in the mountains are anything like the inhabitants of the capital, then surely they'll help him find his son. "It's something Americans can't understand," he tells them. "They are good, simple people who are concerned with their own family and plot of earth."

I read these lines and smart at his hopefulness (and simplification of an entire nation of people), but also marvel at his slight of his own country. The man had spent almost two years as a prisoner of war and marched in countless Memorial Day parades, and here he was, a year after his son's shoot-down, beginning to express a gap in identity that would only widen in the coming years. Then again, I would feel that same closeness to Laos over the home I'd left behind on my trip forty years later. But I'm getting ahead of myself.

The next day is October 14, 1973, thirty years to the exact day Ed's plane was shot down over Germany. It's the day the Royal Lao and Pathet Lao are to release their lists of prisoners. Ed awakens to the sun pouring through the window of his small room in the Lane Xang Hotel. Every anniversary feels different, but finding himself alone in bed on the other side of the world on the day he hoped to learn if his son shared his fate must have been surreal. The coincidence only reinforces his faith that his son will be found.

My grandfather joins the family members of the other missing Americans and they tilt their sunburned faces as they wait for the lists to be read. Ed's feet are swollen—they never stopped bothering him after the winter of '43 and '44 in Stalag 17—pressing up against the hardness of his polished black shoes. I wonder who he is wearing them for: for Jack, maybe; to impress these officials; or to show his colleagues—and himself—that he can hold it together. Years in the military, followed by wearing a state trooper's uniform, have made him a creature of habit. The sun strikes Ed's head at new angles as they all wait for news.

Colonel Soth Petrasi, a high-ranking Pathet Lao diplomat, finally addresses the gathered parents, emphasizing to them that the Paris Peace Agreement did not include provisions for Cambodia, China, or Laos. There will be no list released today. What he says next is stunning, given the circumstances: "It is possible some Americans are being held in remote villages." Petrasi suggests a list of prisoners may be released in a month or two, once the coalition government is more fully established. Ed is elated: "We didn't get the list of prisoners that we wanted, but we were very encouraged by what they told us. This is the first time they've said anything like that."

From Vientiane, my grandfather climbs into a puddle jumper heading south to Savannakhet, metal and glass shaking over the mountains that claimed his son. The airport is little more than a bunker surrounded by mowed grass for the plane to tuck into as it creaks to a stop. Outside the plane, the surrounding mountains are green and thick with growth—the perfect cover to hide a boy. Maybe even his boy.

Jeeps roar up the tarmac in Savannakhet to take passengers to the refugee camp in Seno. My grandfather grips the seat as the tires bounce over red clay roads, the same color as the dirt in Tennessee where his sisters live. The bright dust always caked to his kids' shorts on visits to see their cousins. Here, the clay coats everything, clings to his throat.

Ed can smell the refugee camp before he sees it, all sewage and unfamiliar spices. When the motor stops, the refugees stare at the white man getting out of the jeep. Many members of the Lao military trained with Americans, but the people here are largely civilians, women and children. My grandfather goes to every adult who meets his eyes and hands out headshots of his oldest son.

One man invites Ed into his tent to share homemade beer "which couldn't be refused and incidentally which I thoroughly enjoyed." It is strange to imagine my grandfather in middle age, having survived a war, lost a brother, and with a missing son, still so sure that the world is good, sharing a beer with a refugee from a country his son was bombing. As Ed drinks, his host holds Jack's photograph up to the light, shaking his head before turning back to his own family.

That day at camp is a blur of shaking heads and interviews conducted with gestures and photographs. At one point, it seems like Ed is coming closer to answers: a villager from Sepon in the camp grows excited at a photograph of one of the missing Americans. Ed waits for the interpreter to translate what the man is saying and has to steady himself once he does: the villager tells them that they had buried the man. But when it comes to Jack, the answer is always the same: "Know nothing." Most of the refugees had been evacuated from Sepon years before Jack's shoot-down. Ed is around seventy miles away from the last known place his son was seen alive, but the jeeps he arrived in will take him no closer. *Sepon is not safe. The bombs are everywhere.* The drivers are protecting Ed—Ed, whose son was dropping those bombs.

The ride back to the Savannakhet airport is an eternity of bumps taken at slow speed, any promise of hope the trip held expelled from his lungs.

Before boarding the plane home, my grandfather takes photograph after photograph of the backs of guards at the airport against the blue sky, of the crumbling airstrip, of the mountains in the distance—the closest he can get to his son.

5 / *Prometheus*

We're not looking for a resurrection. We just want the truth.

—**Ed Pearce**

Chiang Mai, Thailand • November 17, 2013 • Mom gone 4 years, 19 days

*R*ed lanterns bounce from strings strung across the moss-covered stones of Tha Pae Gate, the former front door to the northern Thai city of Chiang Mai. My migraine pulses in unison, the colors aggressive and sharp inside my skull. The recycled air of the plane has settled into my lungs like the clouds clinging to the mountains above the city limits, and it's an effort to breathe.

Behind the fortress of ancient brick, giant silk lanterns are stretched into the shapes of elephants, chickens, and horses surrounding technicolor letters spelling out "Sawadee": Hello. It's the second night of Yi Peng, and as Liz and I walk through the gates, meat sizzles upon the spotlit grills of street vendors on Tha Pae Road—sausages on strings and balls of fish wrapped in banana leaves. *I wonder if this is what Grandpa smelled*, I think, recalling his notes about the market in Vientiane. The smoke rises to greet the giant, glowing "S" of a three-story Starbucks, centuries bumping up against one another. Illuminated by the coffee chain's mermaid logo is a multitiered cake of a float crowned with the Thai answer to *Toddlers & Tiaras*: eye-linered mini–beauty queens waving down at us in the green and white light.

Chiang Mai was once part of the kingdom of Lan Xang, the forerunner to modern-day Laos. Roughly translated as the "Land of a Million Elephants," Lan Xang's founder, Fa Ngum, spent 1353 to 1371 conquering parts of what is now Vietnam and northeast Thailand, bringing Theravada Buddhism with him.

Over the centuries, the Thai people fought back, regaining control of Chiang Mai and dominating large swaths of Laos from the late 1700s to the early 1800s. But the Buddhist roots Fa Ngum planted in Thailand remained, paving the way for the celebration we're witnessing tonight.

Liz and I make slow progress down Tha Pae Road. As the smoke from the grills thins, the crowd—and the night—grows thicker, bottlenecking toward Tha Pae Bridge. The air is perfumed with burning lamps but something else, too—the headiness of roses, freshly cut and for sale all along the roads leading to the riverbank.

"We should light one," Liz says.

"Light what?"

"A wreath float."

All day, we've seen people sitting on newspapers outside of stores or by the river, weaving banana leaves and bright flowers into floats called *krathong*. Tonight, they will be set upon the river, a water version of last night's sky-bound ceremony. Many of the roadside stands we walk by now are little more than cardboard boxes set on the sidewalk, all arrayed with startling blooms in every color: sun-yellow marigolds, burgundy roses, royal-purple orchids. I watch the women work and think of my mother's garden—peonies, wisteria, hibiscus, hydrangeas—her hands arranging the cuttings in the clear vase on the kitchen table, the sun coming through the glass. It's hard to imagine expending all of that effort just to let it go.

The closer we get to the bridge, the brighter the paper lanterns rising from its banks glow. To our left, a temple is silhouetted in an indigo-ink sky stitched with fire-white *khom loi*, giving the sensation of staring at an Amish quilt in motion, twinkling and blinking on some celestial laundry line.

I spot a small table set apart from the road and manned by two women with round noses and smiles so similar they have to be mother and daughter. Their offerings are less ornate than the others, but on approach, I can see the attention to detail that has been paid: round "cakes" of banana leaves are tipped with white buds like six-pointed stars, opening to reveal a bundle of fuchsia rosebuds with a single yellow candle at its heart.

When Liz picks one up and hands it to me, it's surprisingly light in my palms. The roses are still fragrant, freshly cut. The petals tickle my fingers.

"How much?" Liz asks.

"Fifty baht."

Liz reaches into her purse before I can stop her and hands over the blue note.

"You didn't have to."

"I wanted to."

"You are ridiculous." I don't bother arguing with her further; she's as stubborn as Mom used to be.

"Tell me more about him," Liz says as we pause on the sidewalk, waiting for a clear path back onto the street.

"About Jack?"

"Yeah."

Last night, I'd told her everything that I'd been able to piece together about my uncle from the accounts of family members and friends since Mom's passing. I know Jack was the big brother who taught his baby brother how to shave, how to hunt with his .22 rifle. That Mom thought his stories around the dinner table were funnier and three times longer than anyone else's, according to uncle Kim—although the thought of a family member even more long-winded than Kim or Mom is hard to buy; when Mom was sick, the two of them would stay on the phone for hours.

"He was a total charmer," I tell Liz as we merge with the foot traffic heading toward the river.

I tell her how, as a teenager, Jack would go out drinking on weekends, meeting his friend Babette behind the Port Jervis, New York, firehouse one town over, where the drinking age was eighteen compared with Pennsylvania's twenty-one. That they used to all call Jack "Kangaroo," because when Babette picked him up in her convertible after a night out at the bars, he always hopped over the trunk and into the back seat instead of using the door.

Liz laughs and tells me she would have liked to meet him.

"Me, too," I say, meaning it.

I tell her what Jim Spier, the only other bachelor in Jack's unit, told me about my uncle: "Jack had a way with girls. He was a smooth talker. In Ohio, there was this bartender in the NCO [noncommissioned officer] club, a superfine-looking lady, who wanted nothing to do with us. Me and Thrasher [another airman] closed the club one night and saw her walk out. Jack was waiting for her in the parking lot. He winked at us as he drove off with her in that yellow Camaro of his."

I try to imagine Jack as Kangaroo in high school, glasses bouncing around his blue eyes as he leaps into the waiting car, laughing with Babette. His face four years later as it looked in his official Air Force photo, the teenage roundness gone, winking at Jim from the Camaro, the car his younger brother still speaks of with awe over forty years after Jack drove away in it toward his second tour of duty and never came back.

Jack Pearce's high school yearbook photo.

"When he returned from his first tour, they say he was different," I tell Liz.

"What do you mean?"

A song I don't recognize is blasting from speakers suspended from a nearby building. It's difficult to hear Liz over the music.

"Jack saw a friend get killed and couldn't get it out of his head."

My uncle Kim had told me the story: "He wanted revenge. I shared a bed with him when he came back. He woke me up in the night swinging and kicking in his sleep and yelling 'fucking gooks.' I woke him up and told him he was dreaming."

Liz and I pause to let a couple pass, their intertwined arms blocking our way forward.

"He was just different. Angry," I tell her.

"A loss like that can change you," Liz says carefully.

I ignore her implication about my own mood and look out toward the water. "I guess so. Whatever it was, he volunteered to go back. He didn't have to—he wanted to."

"I thought everyone was trying to get out of Vietnam."

"All the men in the Sixteenth Special Operations Squadron with Jack were volunteers," I tell her. "But Jack had a personal reason for going back."

For Jack's first tour, he'd been stationed in Da Nang on an old French base that was bustling with U.S. Marines, the Royal Thai Air Force, the U.S. Army, and fellow airmen in 1966. Jack's job code was 46250: a weapons mechanic. He was trained to load guns and bombs on OV-10s. The new planes were specially designed for counterinsurgency combat in the jungle. They could take off on small roads instead of runways and hover during operations. It was Jack's job to make sure the weapons aboard were all in working order, but it wasn't the job he was after: he wanted to be a gunner like his father.

"Jack was miserable," Jim Spier explained to me. "Jack lived and breathed combat. So when he ran into my boss at the NCO club on base, he asked to be a gunner."

Jack's wish was granted and he reported for training in Hurlburt Field, Florida, where he flew choppers for a few months in preparation for combat overseas.

Then everything was taken away from him. The Sixteenth Special Operations Squadron was reassigned from helicopters to slow-moving AC-130s, giant gunships with electronic weapons that dashed Jack's dreams of being a gunner like his father. "The gunners on the AC-130, all we did was load 'em. If they blocked, we'd clear the jam; if they broke, we'd fix it," Jim explained. It was the pilot who actually fired the weapon. Jack was back to where he started before he joined the Sixteenth SOS.

"From the first day Jack arrived in Ubon, he was ragging on the gunners, saying that they were not real gunners, but loader— well—pussies," Jim told me, hesitating to repeat Jack's language to his niece. Ubon Royal Thai Air Force Base in Ratchathani, Thailand, was home to multiple units in 1971, and Jack got along with very few of them.

"Jack drank quite a bit," Jim said. "Once he would get to drinking, that was when it would kick in."

The gunners of the Sixteenth SOS built a makeshift bar in their quarters, moving aside beds on the first floor to construct it. Members bought beer for $2.40 a case and sold it for a quarter a beer, using the profits to hire local women to bartend and keep the beers cold. It was the place they'd all go to blow off steam after tense missions, listen to American music, play cards, swap stories... and fight.

"One night in the gunners' hooch, I thought Olson [Jack's crew chief] was going to kill him," Jim told me. "Jack had been drinking for a while and started ragging Olson, and Olson reached his boiling point and the fight was on. Olson was a tough dude and got the best of Jack and may have done some bad harm to him, but some of the other gunners pulled him off of Jack... Ollie went to our boss, Art Acheson: 'Get him off our crew, or I'll get him.'

"Two days later, Master Sergeant Acheson moved Jack to Smith's crew. I saw Jack in the club eating before his last mission.

I remember he was still griping that he had got a raw deal with Olson. I never discussed this with Jack's mom and dad. They lost a son they loved and it needed to be left alone. I only tell you the truth, because you keep digging into his past and someone is gonna lead you astray and may say some unkind things. I'm not yelling at you and will tell you anything you ask about if I know the facts. Things are not always what they seem. I don't like people spreading misinformation about my gone friends because one lie leads to another one and some are hurtful."

Jack was shot down on his very first night with the new crew. The gunner my uncle replaced that night, Technical Sergeant Sidney Terry, admitted, "Rarely does a day go by that I don't think about that flight. To this day, it puts a lump in my throat because I'm here, and they're not."

"I didn't find out about Jack's dad until after he was gone," Jim told me. "Then everything clicked, then it started making sense about shooting the gun himself."

My mother had tried to stop Jack from returning for a second tour, to convince him that the war was wrong, that he had done his time and should stay home. She wasn't an antiwar activist— with three brothers in the military and a World War II hero father, marching in the streets wasn't an option—but her conversation with her brother was her private, ineffectual protest. Jack was convinced the war was justified and determined to serve: "He kept saying, 'Nobody else wants to go, so I feel I should,'" she told an interviewer in 1977. "He was very strong in his conviction."

All the gunships flying out of Ubon Air Force Base in Thailand were given nicknames. Jack was shot down in "Prometheus," a plane named after the Greek Titan who stole fire from the gods to bring to man. In the myth, Zeus punishes Prometheus by strapping him to a stake on Mount Kaukasos as an eagle feeds on his liver—or, according to some accounts, his heart. But Prometheus can never die; his body regenerates night after night. He's forced to linger in his suffering, not really living and not quite dead.

The river is closer now; I can hear the sound of splashing over the music that's growing fainter behind us. I try to keep up with Liz's bobbing ponytail as she moves through the crowd in the semidarkness. It's as hot as if the sun never went down, the bodies in motion adding to the feverish heat.

"It must have been difficult for your grandparents, to not know if Jack was alive or if he would ever come back," Liz says.

I think of the three years I'd spent dwelling in hope that Mom would make it—hope that was dashed with every test result saying her cancer was advancing—and of the Air Force documents sealed with eagles that tormented my grandparents for decades, each missive swinging them madly from hope to despair.

Liz and I push through the crowd to make our way to the edge of Tha Pae Bridge. The ancient stones are strung with strands of Christmas lights. I put a hand on the cool rock. Below us, people are wading into the river, candles lighting their faces as they set their floats adrift in a constellation of swirling lights, the water Van Gogh's *Starry Night* come to life.

All around us, people are lighting white lanterns. Swaying iPhones and iPads are held up to capture the moments of shaky release and rapid rise. Babies strapped to parents' backs seem to take it all in stride, and one enterprising British couple to our left have equipped their eight-month-old with giant noise-canceling earphones, a comical set of bookends to his bald pink head. Even the baby is staring up at the lights soaring above us. My headache makes my thoughts swirl, a memory from childhood surfacing.

I am four, maybe five, woken from my bed by warm arms—Mom's. Her hands knit themselves around my polyester nightgown, the shiny fabric crackling with static. We meet Dad and my sister in the hall—me in Mom's arms, Morgan a sleepy toddler in Dad's—and we're carried down the stairs still swaddled in quilts. Dad slides the porch door open and the night air hits my face. It smells so different from what it's like during the day, like cut grass and something else—something bigger. The fourteen acres of woods around the house are mostly abandoned pines from a Christmas tree farm gone wild. Mom had fallen in love with this land—*How could you not want to be surrounded by Christmas all year long?* she'd say—and as our parents settle into lawn chairs beneath us, I felt both the enormity of the woods and the warmth of my small family, of Mom holding me close.

"Look up."

There is no human light in sight, just the black edges of the firs and a sky bright with stars. Then one moves. And another.

"Mom, a shooting star!"

"It's a meteor shower, honey."

Morgan claps from her perch on Dad's lap. I'm scared of the size of all this, the way it hangs over our heads. The four of us look up at the streaked sky. I reach for Mom's hand. *Nothing bad can happen to me while she's here.*

"Jess!"

Shit. I've lost her. "Liz?"

"Over here."

A man with thick rings of black around his eyes blinks inches from my face. I step back, nearly stepping on a small child being led through the crowd.

"*Kho thot,* I'm so sorry," I mutter to the stranger.

"Jess!"

I turn and am almost hit by a family of four on a motorcycle, all of them helmetless. I jump back just in time to see Liz's ponytail by the bridge's railing and dive for it.

"You have to stay with me. You scare me when you don't pay attention like that."

I don't know how to explain to Liz where my mind has been going. How this place on the other side of the world is bringing people back to me. How I feel the pull of home.

Home. There is no single place I can identify that way anymore. My life in Brooklyn has been a string of short-term rentals, from a shared apartment in a failed relationship to two Craigslist roommates who are warm but not family. I dream of painting walls, setting down roots, coming home to a kitchen with just my food in the cabinets. My life over the past few years has been an unbroken pattern of office, home, office, home, though I walk faster now to try to block out memories of calling Mom on that last leg of my commute, when I'd linger on the sidewalk to have more time with her voice.

I can stay in Thailand until next month or until my money runs out and it won't matter, because nobody will be waiting up for me. My childhood home is on the market, and soon it won't belong to my family even in title, just as I no longer belong to it. There will never be another night when I listen to the wind in the woods outside my bedroom and think, *But Morgan and Mom and Dad are just down the hall; I'll see them again in the morning.*

In Chiang Mai, empty cups and crushed flowers blanket the patchy grass under my feet. I follow Liz's sneakers as we escape down narrow stone steps cut into the riverbank, the catcalls of ice cream sellers and float makers on the banks above growing distant.

Between the water and us is a stage. On it, dancers lit by firelight move in unison to a slow, sad song played on a flute and guitar. Liz and I skirt the edge of their limelight to reach the lip of the river. Liz borrows a lighter from a pack of teenage girls and hands it to me to light the wick of our float. It sparks blue, then takes, slowly bathing the tiny vessel in light.

I stare into the river and think of what Jack's squadron mate Dave Burns told me about why he returned to Ubon to make Thailand his home after the war: "On the anniversary of every shoot-down, I go to the Moon River in Ubon and I drop a wreath of flowers into the river, because it makes its way to the Mekong in Laos, and that's where my people are. They are no more than five hundred miles away from me. I feel closer to them here than I did in California... I love the United States, but all my heartbreaks and my triumphs and my good and bad memories occurred right here in Asia."

The stone embankment at the water's edge is cold on my knees as I bend to lower the rose-circled candle into the river. It bumps against the stone once, twice, then catches the current and joins the other twinkling points of light slowly expanding and contracting as they bob under the light of the full moon, downstream and out of sight.

I'll later learn that in Buddhist funerals in Laos and Thailand, it is traditional for the family of the deceased to adorn the body with offerings of flowers before taking turns tossing lit incense and candles onto the pyre and watching it burn.

Linda Pearce's passport photo from her Paris trip, 1975.

6 / An American in Paris

The Pentagon doesn't lie. It's a building. It was somebody inside.
—Ed Pearce

Paris, France • April 15, 1975 • Jack missing 3 years, 17 days

*M*om's face is blurry as she stands in her white nightgown, waving from a Parisian balcony. Her strawberry-blond hair is straight and long as it blows across her forehead and out of frame. She's twenty-two and in her first year of teaching high school English, freshly arrived in the French capital for training with fellow teachers from Binghamton, New York. But Mom has another motive for being in Paris.

Everything I know about my mother's trip to Paris is recorded in a few Polaroids, blank postcards that she purchased of Notre Dame, and a long, detailed letter she wrote to her father. It is hard to reconcile the fact that the pictures of her and her friends on a hotel balcony and a bottle of champagne cooling in a bidet came from the same trip as the letter, but I think of my own photos from the past four years (smiling at birthday parties, dancing with friends) and the things they omit (Mom's funeral, packing up the house, lying in bed with the curtains drawn) and begin to understand who my mother was at my age.

Mom arrives at the Vietnamese embassy in Paris at 2:30 in the afternoon on April 15, 1975, in plaid bell-bottoms and without an appointment or the ability to speak a word of French. At five feet six inches, she is solid, if likely shorter than the guards who meet her at the gate, the rise and fall of her chest wide enough for men to take notice. In her purse is a letter from Pennsylvania congress-man Joseph M. McDade and a map of a mountain on the other side of the world, located in a tiny country called Laos.

Vietnam was a French colony from 1887 until 1954, when the communist Viet Minh, led by Ho Chi Minh, beat back French forces at the bloody Battle of Dien Bien Phu. After the victory, the Geneva Accords divided the former colony into the Democratic Republic of Vietnam in the north, run by the Viet Minh and supported by the Soviet Union and China, and the State of Vietnam (later the Republic of Vietnam) in the south, supported by the United States.

Neighboring Laos first became a protectorate of France in 1893 and was subjected to French rule for half a century. To the French, conquering Laos was a means of controlling the Mekong River, a valuable trade route through Southeast Asia, and a place to mine precious metals. France's grasp on the colony first slipped in 1945, when the Japanese occupied Laos in the closing days of World War II. It was lost for good in 1954, when Vietnam was divided and Laos erupted into civil war between the Royal Lao and the communist forces of the Viet Minh–backed Pathet Lao, who smuggled arms and supplies to North Vietnam.

By the time my mother approaches the embassy, Vietnam and Laos are largely in communist hands, the French empire in pieces. My mother knows that every American soldier captured in Laos and returned during Operation Homecoming went through North Vietnamese custody. It is her hope that the Vietnamese ambassador will have more answers for her about Jack than her own government.

For the past three years, my mother has watched her parents shake hands with U.S. senators in front of cameras, American flag pins glinting from the congressmens' lapels, only to have subse-quent calls go unanswered. She has heard the curt professionalism of the Air Force officers trying to assure her father that they are "doing everything they can" to find Jack. But all they really want is for her family to go away, to stay silent. The packet of "rules" sent to the house after her brother was shot down was as thick as a phone book:

> We request that you limit to members of your immediate family discussion of known information concerning your son's status....
>
> [W]e have no objections to your having contact with the press, <u>but it will be your decision to make</u>. However, you should be aware of the very real risk of personal harassment from individuals and/or organizations not in sympathy with our involvement in Southeast Asia and that the effect on prisoner treatment (beneficial or detrimental) cannot be determined with any certainty....
>
> [I]t would be in your best interest not to discuss the situation in terms of national policy or politics as relates to our involvement in Southeast Asia... policy and politics are not germane to the disregard of the Geneva Convention by the enemy.

Because America's involvement in Laos was covert, documentation about what Americans were doing at the time of their loss was highly classified and often beyond the purview of family members. My grandparents were instructed to say Jack's plane was shot down over Southeast Asia instead of Laos if asked. The warnings distributed to families like mine were meant to strike fear into their hearts and prevent the American public from asking too many questions.

My mother does not want to be told what to say, how to think. She does not want a pat on the back and condescending reassurance from another U.S. official. Her father has been taking Jack's story to the press since day one, and she won't be cowed into silence by threats on a piece of paper.

Just days before the Paris Peace Agreement was signed in January 1973, Ed had spoken directly to President Nixon at a National

League of POW/MIA Families convention in Washington, D.C. My grandfather had stood up in front of a roomful of parents and spouses of the missing and asked from among those expectant faces if Laos would be part of the peace treaty, and Nixon had told him, "All of Southeast Asia." His question answered, he'd sat down and watched two parents with sons missing in Cambodia and China ask if the peace agreement would include those countries.

Two more times, Nixon replied, "All of Southeast Asia."

When the Paris Peace Agreement was signed on January 27, 1973, it did not include Laos, Cambodia, or China. Ed had gone to Southeast Asia himself to sort things out and returned empty-handed. Linda was determined to have better luck than her father.

Mom dials Mark Pratt, first secretary of the American embassy in Paris, from her hotel room. When she tells the secretary her father is a former POW and her brother is missing, she gets right through but is denied an appointment with the Vietnamese embassy in Paris because she is "not a representative of her government." When Secretary Pratt offers to host my mother at the embassy and brief her on the situation "personally," she declines. Her brother had been acting on behalf of the U.S. government when his plane was shot down over a neutral country. If he can represent his government, she reasons, so can she.

She records the rest of their conversation in a letter to her father that makes me think, *Mom, how can you feel so confident at the age when I can barely get out of bed with grief for you?*

The address of the Vietnamese embassy in Paris is easy enough for her to find. By three P.M. on April 15, 1975, my mother is sitting across from First Secretary Do Thanh, a man with exaggerated manners and a smile that doesn't seem to leave his face. She is flushed from the long walk, from the audacity of what she has just done, of what she is about to do.

As the two are served tea in the embassy's drawing room, I imagine my mother leaning forward, white hands on the plaid of her lap, describing how her big brother's plane was shot down over the Ho Chi Minh Trail three years and seventeen nights of waiting ago.

Do Thanh nods and smiles, smiles and nods.

She records every detail of the conversation in that letter, admitting she was forced to grow blunt: "Can I bring hope back to my family?"

"I'm afraid, Miss Pearce, that you've come to the wrong place." Do Thanh's tone with her is gentle, as if he were speaking to a confused child. "There are no living American prisoners in Vietnam."

"But, sir—"

"Your brother's crash was in Laos, not Vietnam. Your business is with the Lao embassy."

I can feel my mother's fingers dig into the bone china of her teacup. "I arrived here, sir, because the Americans captured in Laos were all supposedly held in Vietnam."

Do Thanh smiles even wider. When he is sure she is quite done, he inquires if she has had a pleasant stay in Paris. I read this and am reminded of all the men who have seen the blond hair I inherited from my mother and stop short of seeing anything beneath it.

My mother isn't done yet. She coaxes the address of the Lao embassy from Do Thanh's receptionist and marches out one set of gates and through another on Avenue Raymond Poincaré. The Lao woman guarding the entrance doesn't speak English, but my mother shows her the letter from Congressman McDade and is ushered into an inner courtyard of dense green and cool shade.

"Go through that door to the first floor, take the winding staircase, *deuxième étage*," a second attendant tells her.

At the next landing, a young civil servant sends her a floor higher (that confusing French system, with its first floor replaced with *rez-de-chaussée*). By the time she is finished climbing, she is out of breath. The door opens before she can knock. She is face-to-face with Phanthong Phommahaxay, Lao ambassador to France.

My mother takes in the cluttered office behind him. Mr. Phommahaxay steps back to watch the flushed twenty-two-year-old sink into a chair. With her feathered blond fringe and fitted turtleneck, she must have stood out among the slim brunettes of Paris just experimenting with bangs and the Doors.

The letter gives a play-by-play of what was said in that room:

> After explaining why I was there I listened to the man's tirade about the American Aggressors and war mongers.

> *My country just wants to exist as an independent country without interference from others. You overtly make statements of possible friendship, then your C.I.A. trains Thai guerillas to cross the border and gun down motorists upon the highways. Your C.I.A. places bombs in certain buildings, puts poison in Lao cigarettes.*

> I was a little dumbfounded at this information, but stated if this were true, I apologize for my country and I can understand your anger.

> *Your country must show your true and sincere friendship and heal the wounds of war.*

> I asked if "healing the wounds of war" meant money, he agreed that it did... I then asked if there were any prisoners being held in Laos. He repeatedly avoided giving a definite answer. I then inquired about the heavily-forested terrain and the poor communications in his country, which might make it difficult to know the full situation concerning POW/MIAs in his country.

> *I have already contacted local authorities throughout the country and asked them to gather all MIA information in their areas for possible future talks with the U.S.*

I then pushed again about Jack, saying my family believed him to be alive. I explained in detail why we
believed this to be true.

*I find it hard to believe Lao villagers would take anyone
prisoner. Our people are forced into living in caves by
American bombing. They sleep by day and plow by night.
If anyone survived the crash, they would find it difficult
to survive for very long because of starvation and wild
animals.*

I asked if he would have the local authorities search
the area of the crash site and give us any information
they found if I were to supply him with the necessary
crash site information.

I will help anyone who does not believe the war is right.

I replied that a large number of the American population believed the war was a war of the government's
and not of the people. I explained that American men
missing and families were caught in the middle
because Jack and the others had followed their government's orders to fight.

It will be years before the C.I.A.'s clandestine operations in Laos
are fully exposed in the American media, though the press had
already come out with several incendiary stories that went largely
ignored. *The New York Times* ran a story as early as February 1970
suggesting that U.S. involvement in Laos was greater than the
White House was letting on:

President Nixon was reported today to have refused
to authorize the release of anything more than a

heavily censored version of a Senate subcommittee's transcript of Administration testimony on the extent of United States involvement in Laos....

[I]t gives detailed account of American policy and action in Laos, including many facts not previously revealed to the Senate....

Senator Albert Gore, Democrat of Tennessee, told the Senate this week that he had access to the transcript and that the "evidence is ample that the war in Laos and U.S. participation in the war in Laos has been secretly but greatly escalated."

And in April 1971, a televised Senate subcommittee hearing showed Massachusetts senator Edward "Ted" Kennedy, brother of the late president John F. Kennedy and already a celebrity in his own right, questioning former ambassador to Laos William Sullivan about the extent of American bombing in Laos. Kennedy's staffers had traveled to Laos and written a report claiming American planes were targeting civilians. When Sullivan evaded Kennedy's questions, the senator called upon Fred Branfman, an aid worker in Laos who had interviewed hundreds of bombing victims. Branfman's response was broadcast on the evening news: "What I am trying to suggest [is] that the United States has been carrying out the most [heavy] bombing of civilian targets in history."

The revelations did not cause the swell of outrage Kennedy anticipated. Though more Americans were lost in Laos than Cambodia, another focal point of America's containment policy, the bombings in Cambodia garnered far more press, especially after the killing of four Kent State University students at a protest in May 1970. In *A Great Place to Have a War*, author Joshua Kurlantzick writes, "Americans held no massive rallies to protest Laos policy. No huge contingent of antiwar celebrities traveled to Laos to highlight the war there, and no famous musicians held concerts to benefit Laotian refugees or Laotian fighters." I can't help but wonder what would have happened if Mom had reported the ambassador's accusations about American involvement in Laos to journalists back home. If anyone would have believed her or even cared.

On April 29—two weeks after my mother's visit to the Vietnamese and Lao embassies—"White Christmas" plays throughout the streets of Saigon, signaling President Gerald Ford's order for the helicopter evacuation of over seven thousand Americans and South Vietnamese from the capital as communist forces advance. The city is thrown into chaos; footage of crowds surging toward the embassy doors, of women and children being handed into departing helicopters, airs on American television.

At 8:35 A.M. the next day, the last Americans leave Saigon. By 11:00 A.M., President Duong Van Minh's surrender to North Vietnamese troops is broadcast across the world. Van Minh had survived the French colonial occupation of his country and capture by the Japanese in World War II. He will survive this, too, though he will go down in history as the last president of South Vietnam.

Back in Binghamton, my mother mails a package to Mr. Phommahaxay in Paris. It contains a map of her brother's AC-130 crash site that her parents have obtained via a Freedom of Information Act (FOIA) request and a firsthand report of the crash from an eyewitness on the ground that night.

My mother never receives a reply. When I am born almost ten years of waiting later, she will find there is only one song that lulls me to sleep in my crib when I scream and kick and cry: "White Christmas."

Mom will visit me when I am studying abroad in Paris in 2006, when she is about to turn fifty-three—"the big five-three," as she calls it—and I am twenty, just two years shy of the age she was when she knocked on those embassy doors. Her cancer diagnosis lies in wait in the fall. For now, we walk through the French museums I love, and I introduce her to my new friends, show her my new coffee shop, the corner bakery where I can order for her in my new language.

On our last night together, we sit on my dumpy couch in my sixth-floor walk-up apartment, drinking the kind of red wine you buy at Franprix for four euros a pop. The small living room is lit with makeshift candelabras I made by sticking cheap tapers into empty wine bottles. It is the first time I have served my mother dinner, hosted her in a home I have made. Mother's Day, her birthday, and her twenty-seventh wedding anniversary are the following week; my sister has just been accepted to Brandeis for the fall. As we talk, the light jumps up and down the plaster walls of my apartment from the candle wax rushing down the sides of the glass bottles. Mom's eyes are sparkling with wine and candle-light as we make plans together.

"What will your father and I do in that big house all alone?" she asks me.

We talk about her gardening, taking up quilting again, the two of us traveling together once I graduate.

Now, I look back at that moment with her letters in my fist and wonder why she didn't reach across that couch and tell me about her first time in Paris.

7 / *Faith*

Just as America never broke faith with our prisoners of war,
I can assure you today that we shall not break faith with those
who are reported missing in action.
—President Richard Nixon, May 19, 1973

Chiang Mai, Thailand • November 19, 2013 • Mom gone 4 years, 21 days

A chill runs through my wet hair as hundreds of gold banners
turn softly in the breeze from the open doors of Wat Chedi
Luang. Their gilded edges twinkle back at the people below who
had hung them in the hopes of an auspicious year.

Liz and I stoop on the stone steps of the temple to take off
our shoes. I am surprised at the coolness under my toes in the
midmorning heat, the solid feeling of the gently worn stones. The
night before had been a late one. We'd stayed watching until the
last lanterns disappeared from the sky above us and from the water,
the smoke from so many burning wicks turning the riverbank into
a slow-moving cloud.

We step forward into the temple, and as my eyes adjust I nearly
bump into a woman kneeling in front of me. She doesn't notice
the people behind her; her entire being is focused on the tiny
tweezers in her hand. She is applying petals of gold leaf to a statue
of Buddha so bright it resembles a giant, wrapped Easter Bunny.

Liz and I inch forward beneath the soaring ceiling, which
stretches hundreds of feet above the banner canopy. The golden
Buddha in Wat Chedi Luang's altar before us is several stories tall,
gleaming dully in the light from the open door. I crane my neck up

like a child looking at something just out of reach, trying to shake off a feeling so long buried I barely recognize it.

I spent most of my childhood Sundays in St. Ann's Church in West Newbury, Massachusetts. It was a small congregation of young families who stood around after Mass eating stale doughnuts and drinking coffee, but when the candles were lit and my best friend, Jenny, belted out "My God, My God, Why Have You Abandoned Me?" on Good Friday, I *felt* something.

Mom was different. When she married my father, she had taken part in a three-generations-strong Pearce tradition of interfaith marriages: Dad's Catholic to her Methodist. Ed and Rosie were the first generation to break the pattern of boycotting their children's wedding because of "those damn Catholics." Jack was shot down right before Easter 1972, and I had spent every Easter of my childhood with Mom's family.

When Mom got sick, she convinced Dad to return to the Protestant church she had been raised in. Dad and I went to services with her on weekends, both of us stumbling over the different version of the Lord's Prayer. When it was apparent that Mom was *really* sick—still, to us, a temporary state—both the Catholic and the Protestant communities started delivering hot meals to the house and saying prayers for her on Sundays.

Once Mom was confined to bed, an old family friend and member of the Spiritualist church gave her readings from the deceased while she lay propped against pillows, praying to her family like some Catholics pray to saints.

I look up at the altar before me, warmed by the glow from the giant Buddha towering above us. I edge closer to his golden face and study the curve of his lips. Above us, the banners turn as if pulled toward his mysterious smile. It's the most serene smile I've ever seen—and eerily familiar. I stared up at it nightly, I realize, when I stayed in my grandparents' house as a child, in the bedroom that once belonged to my mother.

The set of Buddha bookends Grandpa Ed had brought back from Thailand—bellies round, earlobes dangling—were the last thing I saw when Mom shut the light off at night, the gleam of Buddha's lips staying with me as I drifted off to sleep. I didn't know why Grandpa had gone to Thailand then; I only knew he had brought them back for her.

In a letter to a friend the week after Jack's crash, Mom had alluded to her relationship to her father and his faith: "I know Dad cries at night after Mom has fallen asleep 'cause I've heard him. He and I have had really good talks about life and death, and him and me. I'm glad he's my father." Mom doesn't elaborate on what those views of life and death are or if she ever told her father what she overheard. I'm left imagining my mother lying awake across the hall from her parents at nineteen, observing her father's despair and the gulf between the fear we feel at night and the faith we show our family.

I offer a silent prayer to whoever is listening: *Mom. Grandpa. I'm here. Help.*

As I turn to leave the temple, a monk gestures for me to approach, his lean muscle and the uniform of orange robe making him seem as ageless as the stones that vault above our heads. I kneel on the carpet before him, waiting to see what he'll do next. He leans forward to dip a brush in a bowl once, twice. The bristles emerge dripping. I close my eyes as he sprinkles cold water on my forehead and chants, letting the drops fall down my face. They feel as familiar as rain. I feel his palm on my hand and open my eyes. He's tying a thick white cotton braid around my wrist.

"For luck."

Luck, faith, talismans—I crave anything I can hold on to. The braid is scratchy on my wrist as I place a bill in the alms bowl beside him on the platform. The monk bows slightly, then gestures for me to move forward down the carpet. Liz is behind me, receiving her own bracelet. There are no baptisms in white here; I walked in and felt accepted in a way Mom never was in the church she marched us toward each Sunday. Bitterness rises in me at the memory of leaving Mom behind in the narrow pew as Morgan, Dad, and I walked up to the front of the church to receive Communion. Mom, a Methodist, was forced to stay back and wait.

I think of the ways we define soldiers. Jack's dog tags contained only three forms of information: name, blood type, and religion. EDWIN J. PEARCE. A POS. METHODIST. What would Mom's dog tags say if she had served like her brothers? Her gender had spared her service, but spirituality, like her brother, was something we didn't discuss.

Mom and I talked about the possibility that she could die from the cancer carving out her body exactly once. It was during a rainstorm in the summer of 2009, the last summer of her life.

"Jessica?"

She had called my name from her bedroom, so softly I could just make it out across the upstairs hallway. She often slept in the afternoons now; I'd just popped upstairs to check on her.

"Coming." I retraced my steps and hovered in the doorway to her bedroom, uncomfortable. "Can I let in some light, Mom?"

She nodded and watched me roll the shades up by her bed. When I turned to sit by her, she squinted, as if the dull light was causing her pain. I dropped the shades back down so the only light that fell came through the bottom pane, casting a shadowy checkerboard across the blankets.

"Come sit by me," she said.

I curled up to her right side like I had done thousands of times as a child, adjusting the pillow behind her lower back. I dug my toes under the covers and brushed against her leg. It was dough-soft, her muscles dissolved from a summer of bed rest. She has been sick for almost three years.

Mom smiled and closed her eyes for a minute. I used the rare closeness to study her changing face: a single eyelash held on to a lid and swept a cheek swollen round like the soapy skin of a bubble. She opened her eyes, the blue of them startling against the rose of her steroid-flushed skin. She caught me looking at her and turned away. Her fingers clung to the bed and I realized she was trying to rock herself upward.

"Mom..." I trailed off when she didn't stop. I knew better than to deter her. Her arms shaking, I watched my mother pull herself to a fully seated position and reach for something on her bedside table.

"Your sister is getting the antique pie plate—"

"We don't have to talk about this right now."

"I want you to have something that would be meaningful to you."

"Please—"

"Just listen, Jess."

The breath she took was frightening—deep, as if she were recording the timbre of each particle of air against her throat. Her hand was surprisingly warm against mine when she put the frayed leather slip of a book into it: the pocket-sized book of prayers her father had with him in Stalag 17 prison camp, that kept him going through a forced march through the Austrian Alps. The book that she carried from chemo session to chemo session, that I had seen her read at night when the pain kept her up, the light from her lamp stretching under her bedroom door and into the hallway.

The pages were brittle like a dead fly's wings, the edges beginning to crumble. I read the inscription on the inside flap in faded ink: *To Edwin A. Pearce: "More things are wrought by prayer than this old world dreams of." —Aunt Alice Zaengle.*

Ed Pearce's WWII prayer book from Stalag 17.

The spine cracked in her hands as she turned to a page midway through the small book, where she—or perhaps my grandfather—had underlined a passage: "Fear thou not; for I am with thee: be not dismayed... I will strengthen thee."

"This was my dad's, and it's given me a strength. If one day, you wake up..."

I couldn't look her in the eyes.

"If one day you wake up and I'm not here, I want you to find strength in it, too."

I took it from her and studied the lines in the old leather. When our eyes met again, it was in the mirror across from the bed, where we gave each other the same half smile—the one that says, *Let's be brave about this.*

I held the small book in my hands as the shadows of the trees outside shook across the windowpanes, their black lines crisscrossing the blankets like bars.

I never got the chance to ask my mother if she read that tiny prayer book to be closer to her father or to feel closer to God. We didn't talk about those things. Back then, I wouldn't have known how to ask, anyway.

In Wat Chedi Luang, I pass by the devotee still gilding the small image of Buddha as if every flake were a universe and wish I had her faith. Liz joins me near the entryway to the temple. I look back at the towering Buddha and the woman in prayer, her body as still as Mom's as she waited for her family to come back to her after Communion.

"Ready?" Liz asks.

I can feel the sun on our backs from the open door, hear the sounds of the street coming to life behind us.

"I need a few minutes. I'll meet you out there."

Liz disappears into the bright sun. I look back up at the Buddha and try to pray again, but the prayers won't come. Did Mom close her eyes for the final time expecting to wake up and see her brother and father again? I look up at the rafters with their floating ribbons and see the leaves through the skylight at the hospice, red and orange and gold, the last thing she saw on this earth. *Oh, Mom.* Part of me believed that coming here was a way to show her all of this, of stopping the leaves outside that room from being the end. I want to pull her into the present alongside me, to show her the Buddha's face and bring back the comfort of her childhood bedroom, to show her that she is safe. But I don't know where she is anymore. And I sure as hell don't know how to reach her.

8 / Détente

> The government is trying to close the door and abandon these men.
> We are honor bound to get our men back.
>
> —Ed Pearce

"*D*o you like it?"

The silver bracelet is plain except for a breast cancer awareness ribbon rising where the tip of one cuff meets the other. On the inside of the band is an inscription that would be hidden when worn: *Connecting with courage.*

Mom had bought one for me, one for my sister, and one for herself as a Christmas gift. I resent the way it marks us as a family with cancer, its chin-up mentality that implies we can't be freaked out or in denial. But I don't tell Mom that. Instead, I clamp it on to my wrist as she watches and tell her, "I love it, thank you."

I keep it on as we lie on opposite ends of the couch watching *It's a Wonderful Life*, Mom mouthing all the words she knows by heart before falling asleep, missing her favorite line: "Every time a bell rings an angel gets his wings." I look down as the credits roll to wake her and realize that the raised carving on the bracelet has branded a small pink ribbon into her wrist as she slept.

I began to understand what that bracelet must have meant to my mother only years later, when I found a different cuff bracelet hidden in her sock drawer after her death. While the bracelet she had given me was inscribed with a ribbon, this one bore her brother's name and the date he disappeared: *Edwin J. Pearce, 03/29/72.*

During the Vietnam War, Voices in Vital America manufactured more than five million nickel-plated cuffs with the name, rank, and date of loss of some of the 1,303 soldiers missing in action. The cuffs were not meant to be kept; if the soldier whose name was imprinted on yours returned home, you were supposed to return the bracelet to his family as a thank-you for his service. Mom had worn the band with her brother's name until it had broken in two from use.

Finding that snapped piece of metal made me wonder if buying her daughters a breast cancer bracelet wasn't a way of warding off a conclusive verdict on her disease; as long as the bracelets were worn, we could continue to dwell in hope. Or maybe she liked knowing that one day when she was no longer here, I could look at my wrist and think of her like she once looked down at her own wrist and thought of Jack.

Milford Veterans Home • Milford, Pennsylvania • July 13, 1975
Jack missing 3 years, 3 months, and 14 days

My mother walks behind her parents as the color guard leads them to the slanting white porch of the Milford veterans home. Beside her is her youngest brother, Kim. Her brother's reddish hair falls loosely past his shoulders, as if in defiance of the military cuts all around them. He wears plaid bell-bottoms like hers, the cuffs slowly growing heavy as they drag through the wet grass. My grandmother walks in front of them, holding an umbrella over her white pantsuit as a small crowd gathers in the lightly falling rain. The moment is captured in a photograph on the front page of the *Sunday Herald*, my too-loud family once again the talk of the town.

The previous July, President Nixon and First Lady Pat Nixon, accompanied by Dr. Henry A. Kissinger, had been on an official visit to the Soviet Union to meet with senior officials, an attempt to thaw Cold War relations in the midsummer's heat. Nuclear war, limiting arms, and the situations in Europe, the Middle East, and Indochina were all topics of conversation—even tiny Laos got a mention. To my grandparents, whose son was shot down by a Russian surface-to-air missile, this cooling came too soon and at too great a cost: "What Ed Pearce and relatives of other MIAs want is the U.S. government to use economic power that forces the Russians and Communist Chinese to tell the Pathet Lao, Khmer Rouge, and Viet Cong to account for the missing American servicemen," the *Scranton Tribune* reported.

This July, President Ford is in Helsinki for the Conference on Security and Cooperation in Europe, a further attempt at peace. To Ed and Rosemary, the easing of relations decreases U.S. power to negotiate for the return of missing soldiers. It's a rebuke to their son and the thousands of other soldiers who went to fight Big Bad Communism and never came back: "We could force the Russians who built the SAM that shot our boys down to tell their little ally over there 'Look, the war's over; let's be human and tell the people what happened to their sons,'" my grandfather says. "But they won't. Our leaders and the communist are one and the same. Big money is out to control the world. Kissinger and Nixon sold out."

I had dismissed my grandfather's deep-seated distrust of the Russians to bitterness that his son was lost for a cause his government and the rest of the country seemed to be moving past. Then I learned that in 1974, a Russian returnee from Laos told my grandparents that "there are still Americans being held, some possibly even in Russia," but their source's name wasn't given, the conversation never mentioned again.

I spoke with a C.I.A. officer who was stationed in Laos during the war who shared my grandfather's distrust: "The Vietnamese and the Russians were very close. The Russians were giving them a lot of aid. Did they ever bring in Russians to interrogate downed American pilots? It always bothered us. Would they if they had the chance? Yes. The Vietnamese never wanted to discuss it because they don't want to admit that," Richard Trencher tells me. "Would they have abandoned prisoners at the Hanoi Hilton, would they turn them over to the Russians? Why not? If a Russian KGB officer said, 'Bring us this guy,' and they didn't bring him into the system yet they'd turn him over, no question."

Trencher was twenty-eight years old when he was sent to Laos to win over Lao tribes in the C.I.A.'s fight against communism. He'd just spent four years in neighboring Vietnam and could speak Vietnamese, Thai, Lao, and Russian. Trencher would go from tribe to tribe in the provinces, forming alliances in exchange for weapons and aid. When he returned to Vientiane by helicopter, flying over the jungle hideaways he'd just visited, he would attend sparkling parties with foreign diplomats in the capital. Enemies during the day shared whiskey at night: "In Laos, which was considered a neutral country, we had a Russian embassy, a Chinese embassy, everyone was there. Everyone talked to each other, drank together. It was the Wild West. We all had our own objectives."

There was one objective, however, that everyone seemed to agree on: subverting the 1962 International Agreement on the Neutrality of Laos, which forbid signees like the Soviet Union, China, Vietnam, and the United States from invading or establishing military bases in Laos.

The communists in Laos and Vietnam, Trencher stresses to me, were motivated by a desire for independence, not by a deep-seated belief in communist doctrine like the Russians: "The communists were nationalists, they wanted independence. They didn't want to be part of China. They didn't want to be part of France. They didn't want to be part of America."

Early on, he felt the United States' mission to contain communism in Southeast Asia was doomed to fail: "When I was in Vietnam, the agency didn't think we could win. We figured it out that [those on] our side—the noncommunist side—were totally disorganized and they were highly corrupt against the communist and antigovernment groups. It was just a matter of time before we pulled our aid and they would collapse," he tells me. "The Department of Defense, McNamara, he came out there [to Vietnam] when I was in one of the provinces and I had to brief him. They didn't want to hear reality. The agency sent me to brief the White House... and once we told them 'the agency position is we're not winning, we cannot win,' once we officially had that position, we kept telling him what the situation was. Johnson didn't want to lose the country to communism after China. He was willing to fight and bleed everyone."

The bleeding has stopped, but families like mine are still fighting. The mayor of Milford has declared it "a day of concern for the unreturned prisoners of war and missing in action of America," and my grandfather is being presented with an American flag as a token of thanks for his son's service. In family photos from that day, the perspective shifts from the town paper's lens: Mom stares blankly at the back of her father's wide shoulders, his dark suit jacket wet with rain, as he accepts the folded Stars and Stripes.

The crowd begins to murmur as Ed steps forward with a flag of his own. It is black, the white line drawing at its center the silhouette of a man with a guard tower in the distance behind him. Above his head is written POW*MIA and, beneath it, YOU ARE NOT FORGOTTEN. It's hard not to see Ed at twenty-two in the silhouette, the barbed wire of Stalag 17 above him.

The then four-year-old POW/MIA flag was created by the National League of POW/MIA Families, the group Ed had traveled with to Laos, to raise awareness for loved ones who were still unaccounted for. While it now flies above many state capitols and even the White House, where it is the only flag permitted to be flown other than the American flag, the POW/MIA symbol was then in its infancy.

For Grandpa Ed, the two flags—one for his country and one displaying a horror that was once his and that he now believes to be his son's—are always in balance:

> Only those who have lost their freedom can fully appreciate the true meaning of freedom. As an ex-POW who spent two bitter cold winters in Stalag 17 in World War II, I know the helplessness of being a POW.

Trust in God and America was our only strength and hope. Now as the next of kin of a brave son, who is possibly still alive in a POW camp in Laos, Southeast Asia but abandoned by our own government...I know the shame and even greater helplessness of being an American in a false and apathetic country.

The bells of the Pike County courthouse toll as George Brooks, the father who had accompanied Ed to JCRC headquarters in Thailand, stands before them and speaks: "The White House is afraid to raise the MIA issue because it would upset détente," he says through the rain. "You have to remember that all of our boys were shot down with Russian missiles. They don't make missiles in North Vietnam."

My mother listens to her father's friend, the rain creating a safe wall to protect her from the dozens of eyes staring at her family. After the ceremony, they are supposed to plant a "Freedom Tree" for Jack, a pink dogwood. They have already begun to dig a hole in the mud. The sight of the shovels is upsetting, the shallow space they are digging meant to honor her brother, her brother who is not here.

A document from the Soviet archives from 1972—the year of Jack's crash—will be circulated in the press in 1993. Translated from Vietnamese into Russian and marked "Top Secret," it is written by General Tran Van Quang, deputy chief of staff of the North Vietnamese Army, with instructions to be delivered to the Politburo:

> 1,205 American prisoners of war located in the prisons of North Vietnam—this is a big number. Officially, until now, we published a list of only 368 prisoners of war, the rest we have not revealed. The Government of the U.S.A. knows this well, but it does not know the exact number of prisoners of war, and can only make guesses based on its losses. That is why we are

keeping the number of prisoners of war secret, in accordance with the Politburo's instructions.

Only 591 Americans were released at the end of Operation Homecoming in 1973, meaning more than seven hundred prisoners were held back and never heard from again.

Détente with Russia rules the day, and in November 1975, my grandparents picket the White House with their youngest son and daughter at their side. There is a photo from that protest of my uncle Kim in a cage, his hair grown even wilder; he is now an art student in Philadelphia and has built the mini-prison himself. He clings to its bars as newspaper photographers take his picture and name. Nearby, his parents hold signs with photos of Jack's face and a clear message to the government, captured in the *Times Herald-Record*:

> The words were chilling, at least for them: "Where is Jack Pearce?"... The forty-four months since this event have cut deeply into the Pearces' lives...
>
> "We were never, never the kind of people that would picket the White House," they said, "but the government forced us into this."
>
> They sent Jack off to Vietnam "proudly," just as they sent their two other sons: Bob in the Marines and Mike to the Navy.
>
> Mike's home, and Bob gets his discharge next month. Mrs. Pearce vows "they'll never get another one of my boys back in again."

Four boys, one daughter. Did they pour all that love back into their remaining children, or was there always some that was inaccessible, reserved for a son who never came home? I remember my mother's obsession with taking my sister and me to piano lessons, painting class, and the library after a full day of work and wonder if a part of her wasn't parenting herself. Daughters were a chance at a do-over, her silence about Jack and her illness a way of fulfilling her mother's promise to never let her children be dominated by something beyond their control—or hers.

Kim Pearce protesting in a homemade cage, 1975.

9 / *Lucky*

I want to do something for our grandchildren,
so they'll never have to deal with something like this.
—**Ed Pearce**

Vientiane, Laos • November 20, 2013 • Mom gone 4 years, 22 days

Our first glimpse of Laos is Luang Prabang from the air: brown rivers and mountains misted in indigo and gray. Even from above, the peaks and valleys look like they could swallow you whole.

Jim Spier, Jack's closest friend from Air Force training school, had told me that airmen called flying over the Mekong from Thailand into Laos "crossing the fence"; it was the point where the exterior lights would go dark, the interior of the plane plunged into red—red faces, red weapons, red control panels—to cast less light into the night sky for the enemy. I'd found Jim's name and contact information in my mother's papers and was as shocked as he was when he picked up the phone. Jim told me he was coming off a mission when he ran into Jack in the NCO club on base the night he was shot down, their conversation sticking with him because it was their last:

"I had been in tail 497 that night, area 3 bravo. Real dangerous area. Worked all night long, four-hour mission, destroyed twenty-four trucks, took a lot of ground fire... We were just starting to clean the plane up when the pilot told the nav to give the course to head back home. We were still over the target.

"Before the nav could give us our heading, the BC [Black Crow, a radar system] operator told the pilot, 'I've got a one-ring lock-on'—that meant somebody was looking at us with radar.

"Then: 'I got a two-ringer [surface-to-air missile]! I got a launch light.'

"Our IO [illuminator operator] that night came in over the radio: 'I got two SAM [surface-to-air missile] locks from about six o'clock.'

"I was lying underneath the number two 20 mm disconnecting the drive motor when I was pinned to the floor with G-force. My parachute was close to the right scanner window, out of reach.

"All of the sudden, there was a bright flash of light. One SAM went off below us, the other one three to four hundred feet away.

"There was silence on the radio, then the pilot came through: 'Now, nav, give me that heading.'

"No one talked for fifteen minutes, then someone broke the silence: 'That was pretty damn close.'

"I got off the plane and went straight to the NCO club, and there was Jack.

"'Man, we just came back from 3 bravo.'

"'That's where we're going tonight.'

"'If that's where you're going, wear your parachute.'"

"No parachute?" I broke in. I asked Jim why the hell a trained airman in a plane over enemy territory wouldn't wear something that could save his life.

"We wore a harness with two big hooks in front and kept our parachute close to the foot of our gun so we could grab it, snap it in place, and go. The choice to wear it was left up to the individual, but in fact, you couldn't work and wear the chute. A few guys had worn it a while back and it had opened in the plane."

I tried to estimate the time it would take to stop loading ammunition and reach for the parachute under the gun. *Would there have been time? Did Jack listen?*

"Jack called me, well..."

Jim hesitated on the line, and I waited.

"He called me a pussy, and I told him, 'I'm not kidding you, man. They are not playing games out there.'

"Anyway, that's where they went. I've thought many years about it. It's just luck. Luck of the draw."

There it is again, the one thing my family doesn't seem to have: luck. I twist Mom's ring from Jack on my finger as our plane's wheels hit the airstrip in Laos. Run my fingers across the braided bracelet on my wrist while the runway vibrates beneath the belly of the plane.

The sun is just setting over Luang Prabang as we disembark, but the heat radiating up from the tarmac is so hot it stings the pads of my feet through my flip-flops. Above us, the clouds are pinkening behind the massive peaks that encircle the all but abandoned runway, our plane looking more like a toy than something capable of transporting all the bodies now making their way to the low building housing the "airport." It's little more than a two-story collection of glass, polished to a shine to reflect the surrounding mountains.

Liz swings the door open for me and I spot my face in the glass. The bags underneath my eyes have shrunk. My nose is less congested. I feel stronger in Laos than I did when I first left New York, like everything that has happened to me since happened a long time ago. I shift the weight of my bag stuffed with maps and notebooks, bending to stretch legs cramped from the flight. My ankles poke out from navy-blue capris—I was warned to cover up here, as short shorts are a sign of disrespect.

I turn back toward the plane and let myself fully take in the sky we came from, the sky my grandfather photographed with such care forty years ago and tucked into the family album. When I look at the mountains, I can't help but imagine Jack somewhere among them.

"Next."

I exchange fifty U.S. dollars for a stamp in my passport, and Liz and I are herded into a single room. I see a café and excitedly rush forward—we haven't eaten in hours—but there is only a single tuna sandwich behind the glass, the sputtering fluorescent light highlighting the wet spots where the fish is soaking through the bread.

We are up in the air in another toy plane by 6:06 P.M. The in-flight meal from Luang Prabang to Vientiane comes in a blue box stamped with the Lao Airlines flower and motto: "We are ready to be a Lao National Airline with international standard." Inside is more tuna, this time in a greenish hue and oozing from triangles of crustless white bread.

I leave the sandwich and inhale the pastel pink jelly roll. The accompanying chunks of passion and star fruit cut into ruffled wedges are next, washed down with a water cup sealed with foil. When I turn to Liz, she is delicately peeling back the foil on her water. The rest of her plate is untouched.

"Are you ladies enjoying your meal?" The flight attendant materializes behind Liz, her red nails curled around the back of her seat.

Liz quickly shuts the lid of her blue meal box. "Thanks. It's delicious." Liz's stomach growls audibly as she hands the stewardess her full blue box. I hand my mostly empty one over as well.

"We have to find food," she whispers.

I nod in assent. "Real food."

Liz flips through the guidebook and spends the rest of the short flight reading names of restaurants in Vientiane in a low, sultry voice, the two of us punch-drunk tired and giggling like idiots. The last one describes its wine list in detail. *Yes, this,* we decide.

Night has fallen by the time we touch down in Vientiane. We walk off the plane to baggage claim, little more than a room with a conveyor belt, and see a fortysomething man through the open door opposite, scanning the room. I can't read the sign he holds, but he waves so intensely at us with his free hand that his black hair flops from side to side on his head. As we approach, I can see *Ms. Jessica* has been written on the sign in Sharpie.

His khakis are crisply pleated, the crease down the front ironed with military precision. I'm suddenly aware of how unkempt Liz and I must look in comparison.

"Mr. Bounmith?"

His brown eyes crinkle as he smiles. He nods. "Miss Jessica?"

"Yes. That's me. And this is Liz."

He turns to Liz and bows slightly. "*Saibaidee.* Welcome to Laos."

The Lao greeting is nearly identical to the Thai, but the pronunciation is different, the second syllable more like our "bye." The syllable sinks through me, a clear reminder that I've left the general comfort of Thailand and am in the country where my grandfather was turned away from his final destination. There are no tourists with cameras and shorts here. We are the only white people in the airport.

"Please, this way."

Mr. Bounmith grabs both of our bags from us as if they were full of air and rolls them out into the warm night. All we can do is follow as he loads them into his car.

A good friend of mine in Brooklyn connected us to Mr. Bounmith. His childhood friend Tan is from Laos and recently returned to teach there. When Tan heard that two girls from New York were coming to Vientiane, he graciously offered his home and driver, Mr. Bounmith, to us. I was shocked that a stranger could be so welcoming, especially given my family's history. Tan and I had corresponded via email for weeks, talking about our hometowns and the history of Laos. I was hoping to meet him, take him out for meals, and learn more about his city. But he will be on a field trip with his students during our visit.

"I'm sorry that we won't get to meet Mr. Tan," I say to Mr. Bounmith.

He nods. "He regrets this, too. But I assure you, you'll enjoy your stay in Vientiane." He opens the car door for us like we're royalty, his head bowed slightly to reveal a perfect part.

"We're definitely not in Brooklyn anymore," I whisper to Liz as we slide into the back seat.

The engine starts, and we are on our way to the capital. As we speed into the city, I catch a blurred glimpse of a giant, illuminated arch in the dark. "Patuxai Gate!"

Mr. Bounmith smiles, as if pleased that I recognized the local attraction. The monumental arch was built in the 1960s to honor those who died in the name of Lao independence, though it's modeled after the Arc de Triomphe of their former French colonizers and the concrete it was poured from was bought with American money meant for constructing a new airport.

We drive down Fa Ngum Road, the Mekong silver with the headlights of cars and the full moon, big and close, beside us. I roll down the window. A cool breeze mixed with gasoline and sweat presses our cheeks as the sound of hundreds of small motors purr in the dark.

At a stoplight, we turn away from the river, and the roads and restaurants begin to shrink behind us. Motorcycles fly by, families and couples leaning into each turn together. It's just like Chiang Mai but with one small difference: "They wear helmets here," Mr. Bounmith explains, "or face a large fine."

We drive past French-style estates hidden behind massive stone gates and palms. The car passes a giant, illuminated mansion on a hill, and Liz and I both form the question: "Who—?"

"President," Mr. Bounmith says with a laugh. "Like your Mr. Obama's house."

Like the White House if it were lit like Las Vegas.

We turn off into increasingly modest streets and take a left, passing a French restaurant whose black iron curlicue chairs are all but abandoned except for a stray cat hopping between them, before arriving at a locked gate. The iron entrance faces a dirt road lined with similar high gates and palm trees that disappear down the bend in the road. Mr. Bounmith makes a call on a large flip phone, and I hear a dog barking from behind the fence.

A hand appears and swings the gate open, revealing a stout smiling woman in her forties, her blue-black hair in a ponytail that falls down to her waist.

"*Saibaidee*. Welcome! You must be Miss Jessica and Miss Elizabeth. I'm Vieng."

Vieng, Tan's housekeeper. He had mentioned her in emails, said she'd take care of anything we needed in his absence. Behind her, a black dog barks wildly by the porch, unsure of us. Vieng alternates between smiling at us and turning to yell, "*Beau! Beau!*" at the skinny, skittish mutt.

Mr. Bounmith pulls the car into the driveway and Vieng immediately snaps the gate shut behind us. The closing echoes, making me jump. *That was quick.*

We get out of the car and shake Vieng's offered hand.

"Welcome, welcome. Mr. Tan is sorry that he cannot be here but has asked that I give a tour to his guests."

She reaches around me to grab my suitcase handle and leads us to the door, turns, and stares at my shoes. I see the perfectly lined-up row of slippers by the door and sheepishly slide off my sandals. Liz follows suit.

Vieng smiles at us approvingly. "This way."

Tan's house is all wide floorboards shining under high ceilings and white walls. An oscillating fan blows across an understated dining table, bare except for a woven table runner underneath a blinking laptop. On the far wall is a wicker couch and chair beneath a framed poster of a Degas ballerina. Vieng shows us to the guest room on the right (Liz's) and Tan's room on the left (mine). We stand in the hallway, practically dumbfounded that we have our own rooms. *Our own rooms!*

Vieng looks from American to American. "If you'd prefer to sleep together..."

We giggle and say we are happy to have our own spaces, though once I roll my suitcase beside the teak bed and unfamiliar dresser, I feel a twinge of sadness, aloneness setting in.

Mr. Bounmith has agreed to drive us to dinner, so I shake it off and hurry to dress, slipping on fresh black pants before meeting Liz back at the car. She's changed into khakis and a green shirt that brings out the brightness of her eyes.

"I've been wearing the same thing for two days," she says, seeing the look on my face. "I figured it was time for a change."

Clearly, we're both more than a little bit excited for dinner.

Fa Ngum Road is a ribbon of red taillights as it winds along the Mekong.

"Over there is Thailand," Mr. Bounmith says, pointing to the opposite bank. It seems like you could just paddle a boat for five minutes and be there. I picture Jack's plane passing overhead all those years ago, the interior lights switching to red as he crossed from one country's airspace into another's.

As I look out the car window, I see mother and daughter pairs dipping into the shops that line the riverbank, complete families piling onto mopeds to head home to family meals. Sure, I don't know what's waiting for them at home or what their relationships are really like. But in that moment, the thought comes unbidden: *Lucky.*

Liz and I exit the car at Rue François Ngin, and as we step out onto the sidewalk, I suddenly feel like I'm back home in New York, somewhere on the streets of SoHo. Tiny cafés and restaurants with eaves strung with white lights greet us. The scent of *naem khao*, the Vientiane specialty of pigskin, ground pork, scrambled eggs, and curry paste over rice, drifts into the night air. My stomach calls audibly in response.

We are greeted by a tall maître d' and seated at the front of the restaurant's tiled sidewalk deck. Waiters immediately descend and spread large food menus in front of our faces. One of them lights a votive candle, smoke from the match twisting up into the moonlight. We order heaping plates of *larb* and steaming hot *mok pa*, mounds of *khao niew* and a whole fish stuffed with chili and lemongrass. When our waiter asks if we want a bottle to split, I assume he means water, as every other meal has involved this question. He returns with a bottle of Chianti and two generously shaped wine goblets. I look at Liz and she looks right back at me.

"I'm in if you are," she says.

It's my first night of breathing through my nose without the aid of cold medicine. It's also our first night in Laos. *Why not?* I nod and watch the red liquid slosh into our cups as our waiter pours the wine.

Liz and I raise our glasses in the humid air. Behind us, I can see Mr. Bounmith sitting on a wicker chair at the bar across the street, chatting with other men who seem to come and go—judging by the keys dangling from their hands, other drivers, rendezvousing before returning to their patrons. He does not play with a smartphone or do a crossword puzzle; he sits, facing the road, not meeting our gaze.

"To Jack," Liz says, pulling me from my thoughts.

"To Jack," I agree, clinking.

I drink deeply, the wine coating my still-sore throat.

"What do you want to find out there?" Liz gestures at the blackness beyond our table, in the direction of the mountains.

I look from the sky to my glass. "I want to know what really happened to Jack that night after his plane went down. Whether or not the rumors of Americans being held prisoner in Laos were true."

Before leaving on the trip, I had made contact with Rosemary Conway, who was a thirty-five-year-old schoolteacher at the USAID compound in Vientiane in June 1975 when she was imprisoned by the Pathet Lao and accused of spying for the CIA. Her capture was recorded as far away as the *Seattle Spokesman-Review* and *The New York Times*, the latter of which reported:

> The Pathet Lao accused the Central Intelligence Agency today of continued involvement in Laos and warned that the United States Embassy would bear the consequences of what it termed "sabotage."
>
> The Pathet Lao radio charged in a broadcast that Rosemary Ann Conway, 35 years old, of San Jose, Calif., and Chicago, was a C.I.A. agent who had tried to induce Laotian Air Force personnel to fly T-28

fighter-bombers—provided under United States military aid—out of the country.

The police have held Miss Conway in Vientiane since June 5...

Police sources said she has been undergoing questioning by Pathet Lao representatives of the joint police force, made up of Communists and non-Communists...

It charged that she offered a large sum of money to the air force officers and men so as to buy them off to fly T-28's to an American base in Thailand once used by the C.I.A. to train recruits for its "secret army" in Laos.

On the phone with me, Conway confirmed the allegations that she was, in fact, a contractor for the C.I.A. who had gotten "millions of dollars' worth of planes" out of Laos. "The C.I.A. owned all the airplanes in the Lao air force," she explained to me, adding, "It was my job to get them out at the end. My job to get the Lao pilots out." The June 12, 1975, Pathet Lao daily bulletin and the *Vientiane Post* reported that she had been traveling between Laos and Cambodia since 1974 carrying out C.I.A. intelligence missions.

While in custody in Vientiane, Conway told me she overheard guards who did not realize how well she spoke Lao mentioning the names of American prisoners and the locations they were being held. "When I was in prison, the communists said they would send me to Sepon," she told me—the village Jack was bombing the night he was shot down. "They said, 'You like pilots so much? We're going to send you to Sepon.' I knew how remote that was. I know my way all around Laos and Thailand, I've been on every single base we had in Southeast Asia. They were going to put me in with the prisoners that would include your uncle."

To dissuade her captors from transferring her to Sepon, Conway told them they wouldn't get much money for her. "The

French always paid [for hostages]," she explained to me, "so they expected they were getting money for me. They did—$1.2 million— but that came from Langley, Virginia, not the government. I was fortunate."

Fortunate indeed. An Australian press photographer took her picture while she was incarcerated, drawing international scrutiny... and the concern of Australia's Department of Foreign Affairs, who wrote in a telegram to Secretary of State Kissinger: "The case of Ms. Rosemary Conway has become the subject of considerable local press interest... We will defer next approach [attempted rescue] until June 16 in hope that sensationalism which now attaches to this case will have diminished."

While the C.I.A. later attempted to discredit Conway, her testimony that prisoners were still alive in Laos is corroborated by other live sighting reports I had compiled over the years. One of the soldiers Conway overheard her guards discussing was Morgan Jefferson Donahue, a member of the 606th Special Operations Squadron who disappeared over Laos in 1969. Conway believed Donahue was one of the men imprisoned in Sepon—information later supported by a Lao resistance group that claimed six men were being held in a cave there and forced to repair captured U.S. equipment.

In October 1987, a Lao refugee in Thailand provided information on two American prisoners: Donahue and an "HP St. Phenson," sharing their corresponding service numbers, ranks, religions, and blood types. The information on "St. Phenson" corresponded to Howard D. Stephenson, a crew member on Jack's plane the night it was shot down. The source also said "St. Phenson" had made two unsuccessful attempts to escape. Stephenson was allegedly spotted alive in 1987 at the same prison, guarded, the source said, by Vietnamese soldiers.

If I can just find someone in Sepon willing to talk to me, then maybe, just maybe, they'll be able to tell me what happened to Jack, Howard Stephenson, and the twelve airmen who went down with them. If any of them were really captured alive.

"I want to find someone who was in the village the night of the attack. I've heard so much from the Air Force's side," I start to tell Liz. I think of the official reports, their clinical discussion of beeper signals, air speeds, and probabilities. "I want to know what it felt like for those families on the ground, the ones being bombed."

My family could eat TV dinners and outwardly go on with our lives; the Lao were still living in homes pocked by bombs. War heroes from that time are on their currency. Their grief could not be private because it was woven into the very fabric of their lives.

"Do you think we can find people willing to talk to us?" Liz asks.

Late at night in the months before the trip, I'd fantasized that enough time had passed that sharing knowledge about missing soldiers was no longer a threat. That the people I was traveling thousands of miles to meet would tell me things the Air Force could not tell my grandfather, answer questions my mom died not knowing the answers to. I pictured myself marching through the jungle, taking notes on local customs and the Pantone shades of mountains, gathering data like I did during the days I'd accompany Mom to the hospital, asking questions about recovery rates and side effects, the facts a barrier shielding me from the crumpled look on Mom's face when she received bad news. Her eyes would darken for a moment before she'd recover enough to twist her face back into a smile for her waiting daughter.

Now that I'm here, the litany of dates and facts I had studied for so long waver in the wet heat of Vientiane. I let the vision of the lanterns drifting off into the sky press into my memory. *Breathe.*

"I don't know. I'm nervous."

"It's okay to be nervous. Even if you don't find out anything your grandfather didn't already know—and, Jess, it's likely you won't—it's incredible that you came here. That you're following in the footsteps of your grandfather. He'd be so proud of you. Your mom, too."

Proud of you. I'd spent so much time after Mom's death acting as if she could somehow see me. Those nights alone in the apartment in Brooklyn, washing dishes in the sink with her face reflected back at me in the window, scrubbing until my hands were red from the scalding water. The hours put in at the office, staring at a screen, an editor like she always wanted to be. To hear it spoken aloud in the world, my most private wish, makes my breath catch in my throat.

"I don't know how to thank you for coming on this trip with me," I manage to whisper. "It means the world to me that you're here."

Liz reaches across the table and puts her hand on my shoulder. "Of course I'm here."

Our waiter arrives with our food, and Liz and I pause our conversation again as he stands before us, waiting for us to compliment his presentation. I look down at the raw pink *larb* and the cooked eyes of the chili-stuffed fish staring up at me and feel my stomach churn, my nerves ruining the appetite that nearly consumed me on the plane. I nod up at our waiter and smile but can feel the falseness of the gesture in my very cheeks. He must have, too, because he gives a slight bow and leaves us.

Liz pours me more wine, and I watch it thunder into the glass.

Most of the patrons have left the restaurant by the time our bottle is empty, my plate slivers of fish bones and sticky rice. It's just a British couple, presumably driven here by the man sitting next to Mr. Bounmith across the street, and us. Self-conscious, I ask our waiter for the check.

The city blurs by on the drive home. We take a right at Thongkang Coffee Shop and pass the fancy French restaurant before pulling up at Tan's twenty-foot-high locked gate.

"Thank you, Mr. Bounmith. See you tomorrow? Eight thirty?" I ask.

"Yes." He nods in silhouette from the driver's seat as Liz and I exit the car. He stays put, the headlights shining on the locked gate whose fence entirely surrounds the property.

For the second time, I feel uneasy. *What are these locked gates designed to keep out?* Liz walks a bit unsteadily toward it, bending down in the dark to turn the key. The gate groans but doesn't budge.

She gives it a jerk, the iron shrieking. Locked. A car door opens and Mr. Bounmith is beside us, his body blocking the headlights. He's so close I can feel his breath on my neck.

"Excuse me."

Liz and I step back in unison as he leans against the gate, reaching his entire arm through a small hole in the door in an attempt to jigger the jammed lock. Tan's dog, Beau, is barking now, his white teeth visible in the dark behind the gate. We try again but it's no use; something is stuck. Mr. Bounmith disappears back into his car and I see the blue flare of a cell phone.

Within moments, a distant motor cuts through the night air, growing louder as it echoes down the walled lane. Vieng appears around the bend astride a motorcycle in a nightgown, her long hair streaming behind her. Her tires kick up a cloud of dust that rises to mingle with the gates of the locked, dark homes she passes.

She dismounts a few feet in front of us and approaches the gate. It sighs and swings open on Vieng's first try. Beau stops barking the minute she pats his head.

"I'm sorry for waking you," I say.

"It is nothing. You are guests here. You are welcome."

She nods to Mr. Bounmith, and he gets back into his car and starts the engine.

Vieng shoos us into the yard, then swings the gate shut with a moan between us, locking us in. The last thing I see is the white of her nightgown as she remounts her motorcycle and flies down the lane toward home.

Inside Tan's house, the air is close and warm. I say good night to Liz in the hallway and enter Tan's bedroom. It's my first night alone in a bed, let alone a room, in days. The unfamiliar furniture in the corners glow vivid shades of blue as I undress and climb into bed, the room spinning around me in the dark.

Through the open window, the sound of a neighbor singing "Happy Birthday" wafts into the room, the English words strange on his lips.

10 / The Rallier

We don't want to accept it and then find him
suffering in a prison camp somewhere.
—Linda Pearce Rotondi

Binghamton, New York • July 24, 1976
Jack missing 4 years, 3 months, and 25 days

*M*y mother is twenty-three years old when my grandmother
calls to tell her that the Air Force covered up what happened
to Jack's crew the night of the crash. I picture Mom standing by the
window of her first apartment in Binghamton in the heat of July, a
fan blowing across her fingers as she coils and uncoils the phone
cord, her mother's sobs coming through the line like hiccups. She
isn't sure how to stop them, how to soothe the woman who has
always been unflappable in front of her children. She repeatedly
tells my grandmother to calm down, to slow down, to say it again.

Rosemary is calling from the National League of POW/MIA
Families convention at the Statler Hilton hotel in Washington, D.C.
The annual gathering is one of the few events where the government meets the families of the missing halfway, allowing them
access to Air Force officials and documents placed in the case files
of MIA soldiers. And what her mother is saying, if true, changes
all of their hopes for Jack.

In July, my grandfather retired from the Pennsylvania State
Police after thirty years of service to devote himself full-time to the
search. He is fifty-four years old. Ed has risen through the ranks
to become the Northeast coordinator for the National League of

POW/MIA Families and state MIA chairman for the Veterans of Foreign Wars. He drives across highways to speak at Elk Lodges and VFW posts and parades, crisscrossing New England and dipping into small towns in Pennsylvania and New York. At each stop, other veterans gather around him, asking him to talk about his experience as a prisoner of war. They want to know what it was like to jump out of a burning plane, what he saw crossing the Alps on foot as the Germans fled. Instead, he talks about his missing son and the need to bring America's boys home from Vietnam and Laos. *Father and son, both shot down, son still missing.* The local papers love it.

My grandmother accompanies him to each stop, writing letters to statesmen and fellow families of the missing after supper or from the road, reading them aloud to Ed before sealing them and sending them off across state lines.

It is over those state lines, from Rosie's hotel room in Washington, D.C., to Mom's apartment in upstate New York, that the most incredible chapter of Jack's story begins. What my grandmother told Mom that day is recorded with precision in a memo my grandmother later circulated to the press and elected officials, her account of conversations with Air Force personnel so damning that a colonel felt the need to respond. I read it now and see the day from her point of view, a mother with a missing son refusing to give up.

The echoing grand ballroom of the Statler Hilton is packed with American flags to greet the families of the missing. My grandmother stands among them, shifting from foot to foot. If she had her way, she'd be in flats, but she is in the city now, and these uniformed men require height to stand up to. She is five foot two, and all five feet four inches of her in heels has been standing in line to receive her son's case file from the Air Force for over an hour.

"Next."

My grandmother steps forward and gives her son's name. The officer disappears and reemerges with a thin manila folder—Jack's personnel file. The families are allowed access to them only under supervision. Rosie grabs it from him and seats herself at a nearby table, bringing along her third cup of coffee. I see her there, the raspberry lipstick she always wore stuck to the rim of her cup, steadying herself before opening the folder. It contains photocopies of Jack's passport, loss report... nothing she hasn't seen. She flips through pages so familiar, she could have recited them verbatim. No news. Again.

She makes herself stand up and hand the file back.

"Rosemary! Is that you?"

My grandmother turns and sees her friend Betty Castillo approaching. Betty's husband, Richard, was on Jack's plane the night of the crash. Though the women are a generation apart, they've become fast friends, corresponding at first through the Air Force in the days after the shoot-down, then directly and in warmer tones, their letters evolving from shared loss reports to family recipes and bits of dark humor. Rosie hasn't seen her friend in months, and today, she barely recognizes her—Betty looks as if she's ready to somersault across the floor, heels and all.

She pulls Rosemary into a hug. "I can't believe it! Can you?"

"Believe what?"

The din around them in the Statler Hilton's grand ballroom is so loud that Rosemary has to lean forward to hear Betty's reply.

"The eyewitness report. That a Lao soldier *saw* the plane go down and saw..."

Betty's voice shakes. She gestures to two of the folding chairs that have been hastily set up around the room. Rosie sits down beside her friend.

"Saw what, Betty?"

"That report that said an enemy witness saw nine of our crew members rescued by civilians."

Rescued? The echoing conference hall around them with its tables and speakers and programs shrinks to nothing and falls away.

At the past few conventions, the speeches from Air Force personnel meant to reassure Rosie only worsened the nightmares that came when she returned home to face an oven dormant on her son's birthday. Betty's news, if true, is the biggest slice of hope they've been handed since the crash.

My grandmother blinks at Betty, wondering if she's heard her correctly. There was no such document in Jack's file. She asks Betty to show her the report. Betty nods, excited. The two women march side by side to where Rosie had stood what seems like lifetimes before, her lipstick-stained coffee cup the only sign it has been mere minutes. The world is different, cast in Air Force blue and open sky and *nine survivors* jumping toward rescue.

The line has dwindled, and only a few family members mill around. Betty approaches an officer standing by the boxes of documents and asks for Richard's paperwork.

The man disappears into a back room and returns with the file. Rosie leans over Betty's shoulder as she flips through it. The contents of the manila folder are nearly identical to the one Rosie had been given about Jack. It makes the same *thud* when placed on a table; turning the pages lets out the same rustle as the papers she'd requested from the government via the Freedom of Information Act, the pages largely blacked out and useless to her.

"It was in here a minute ago, I swear."

My grandmother tells Betty to take her time, though it's taking everything she has not to flip through the folder herself.

"It's not here," Betty whispers.

"What?"

"It's not here."

Betty's face reddens at each desperate turn of the page that doesn't reveal the missing report.

"I swear I saw it, Rosie."

"I believe you."

My grandmother looks from her friend to the Air Force officer who had handed them the file. He is standing fifteen feet way, avoiding all eye contact. She hustles toward the officer, giving me visions of her grabbing him by his muscled shoulders and shaking him the way she would shake out the rag rugs against the side of her house in Milford, her five children scattering at her feet. Instead, she pauses and asks the officer point-blank, "What did you do with the eyewitness report that was in here this morning?"

He avoids her eyes a second time as he responds: "The paper has been lost."

He didn't ask which paper. He didn't act confused. He *knew*. Knew exactly what they were talking about. Rosemary is so upset, she neglects to read his nameplate—not a mistake a state trooper's wife makes often.

"The paper has been destroyed," another voice barks from the doorway.

The women turn to see a second officer approaching. The silver tag on his chest is inscribed CAPTAIN HAWKS.

"Captain Hawks, is it?" Rosemary starts. "I never..."

The room shatters into the shouting of a wife and a mother of the missing.

"Ma'am, I think I have what you're looking for."

The deep voice comes from a man who'd entered the room so silently it was as if he slipped in with the heat of the July air. Rosemary's eyes rest on the golden oak leaf pinned to his chest. A major. The nameplate below says SILVERBRUSH. Major Silverbrush reaches into a briefcase and hands Betty a single piece of paper. It looks like any other of the countless onionskin-colored sheets collated in the missing men's manila case files. You could even call it nondescript if it weren't for the fact that none of the other wives and mothers of the men on Jack's plane had ever seen it before.

Betty gives the sheet to Rosemary so she can read the single paragraph keyed by typewriter. It barely takes up half a page, but each line sends ice into her bones:

> At approx. 2100H on 30 March 72... near 38th MIL
> station Savannakhet (P), Laos, a NVA convoy... of
> trucks... moved on the road between the 35th to 38th

MIL stations. The 38th station informed [them] of enemy ACFT [aircraft] (one C-130 [Jack's] and two F-4 jet fighters) approaching from the south... The convoy then was bombed by the C-130 ACFT which made five passes. Source obsr [observed] some of the trucks burning after first three bomb passes. On the fourth pass, source OBSR three other trucks being hit and catching fire. On the fifth pass, the ACFT was hit by 37 MM AA fire... The ACFT caught fire, turned southward and crashed approx. 10 KM south... The 38 station pers [personnel] (except source who stayed at the station) rushed to the crash site. When the PERS returned to the station they told source that they had only OBSR the wreckage and that the *nine crew-members of the downed ACFT had been rescued by Laotian civilians living near the crash site.*

More damning are the handwritten notes in the margins: "Ramsower plus thirteen" and "Curtis Miller." Ramsower was the commander of Jack's plane that night and Curtis Miller was the pilot. Fourteen men lost. Seeing a human hand, those familiar names carelessly scribbled across the document, was an insult. They'd been looking for four years. *Four years.* And this was the first time they'd heard that someone had seen the wreck when it was still hot. Smoking. Had seen nine boys pulled out of it. Maybe *their* boys.

"Major Silverbrush, I'd like a copy of this... this... document for my son's file," Rosie says.

"I'm afraid that's not possible."

My grandmother bristles. "The hotel has a copying machine. I assure you it's very possible."

"I can't let you do that."

My grandmother glances around at the tables, the boxes... and a stack of blank sheets. "Then let me copy it by hand."

Without asking for permission, she walks over to the stack of paper and grabs a handful like she'd later grab napkins from fast-food chains before stuffing them in her purse.

"Surely you won't object if I take a few notes, Major?" She pulls her pen from her purse, holds it suspended in the air.

I picture Rosie's eyes meeting Silverbrush's. For a few endless seconds, no one speaks.

"Be my guest." He turns to leave.

"And I want a copy of this placed in every man's folder on my son's plane."

The "Rallier's Report," with notes in Rosemary's handwriting.

Major Silverbrush pauses and turns to Betty and Rosie, taking the measure of each woman. He nods. My grandmother copies the typed paragraph swiftly, then the handwritten notations containing crewmen's names and strings of numbers and letters—dates? classification codes?—that curl around the margins.

It will be months before Randolph Air Force Base sends her a typed copy of what it refers to as the "Rallier's Report," or spy's report, now in her hands. But the incriminating handwritten notations are missing, the crew members' names sanitized from the margins.

She'll write her own report that she distributes to the National League of POW/MIA Families and the press: "If this paper was so insignificant as they would have us believe, why all the LIES?"

Major Silverbrush's letter in response is swift. He says the Air Force cannot be sure the report pertained to Jack's plane. But Jack's plane was the first AC-130 lost in two years, and when another AC-130 was shot down the next day, all men aboard were rescued.

Rosemary, true to form, replies, "How many AC-130s do you lose in a day?"

Silverbrush persists in his efforts to diminish the report. He claims the source that wrote it was an F-6: Air Force–speak for an unreliable source. Another reason to discount its authenticity. Not to Rosie. My grandmother files a FOIA request so she can see for herself just what the Air Force knows—or doesn't know—about the crash. When it arrives, she uncovers that the source quoted in the eyewitness report was not an F-6 like Major Silverbrush claimed but a B-2, or "highly reliable" source, who provided information on ten other POWs captured in Laos, including a Navy pilot who was one of the "Laos Nine" safely returned home during Operation Homecoming. She fires off a statement to the press: "I would say the Air Force is a shining example of an F-6."

My mother takes up my grandmother's crusade in 1977, writing the letter to President Carter I found the day she died. As I reread it, the anger of a mother and daughter transfers to the granddaughter holding it, their frustration fusing with mine. Only

I'm not just upset at the Air Force on their behalf; I'm upset at the women who kept it all a secret from me. Why didn't Mom and I talk about the fact that she lost Jack at the same age Morgan and I were losing her?

While the president never responds to my mother, Colonel A. W. Gratch, USAF assistant for casualty matters, does. The thick streaks of graphite pressed beneath the passages my mother underlined are my only clues to how she felt about the letter:

June 8, 1977

Dear Ms. Pearce,

On behalf of President Carter, I am replying to your letter of 30 April 1977 regarding your brother, Senior Master Sergeant Edwin J. Pearce....

The aircraft appeared to one witness to be tumbling. This is a severe aircraft maneuver and would almost positively preclude the donning of a parachute, let alone making one's way to an exit to bail out. Indeed, the chance that anyone survived the crash of your brother's aircraft is minimal.

The D.I.A. report which you mention was later clarified to state that the source's information that nine crewmembers on the aircraft were rescued by Laotian civilians was considered untrue as none of the crewmembers returned....

It has never been our wish nor our intent to convey hope where little exists. Many men were continued in a missing status, even though the circumstances of their loss were grim and the probability of survival was remote, for what was thought to be the best interest of the missing personnel.

When the conflict ended our repatriated prisoners of war were debriefed. As a result of their information, coupled with all known intelligence data, and official statements from the <u>North Vietnam government that all prisoners had been returned</u>, it was concluded that none of our men were left alive and held against their will in Indochina....

We can surely understand your intense desire for an accounting of your brother; it is our sincere wish as well. The anguish that has been yours throughout the long period of time since Senior Master Sergeant Pearce became missing has been shared by us on behalf of all of the Air Force personnel lost for which no specific information has ever been received.

Sincerely,
A.W. Gratch, Colonel, USAF, Asst for Casualty Matters

I don't know if Mom called her parents after reading this or if she waited to gather her thoughts. I have to imagine her doing what she always did when she needed to clear her head: drive. I picture her in the driver's seat of her navy-blue Triumph Spitfire, a hand-me-down from her brother when he was last home on leave, clutching the steering wheel like she clutched the lapels of Jack's dress blues before he left for his second tour of duty and never came back.

11 / *American Imperialists*

When a country doesn't have any honor, like a man who
doesn't have any honor, then it's a shell.
—Rosemary Pearce

Vientiane, Laos • November 21, 2013 • Mom gone 4 years, 23 days

When I wake up at seven A.M., Liz is already outside on the
porch, eyes closed to the sun. Her blue eyes pop open at
my approach. "Morning."

Beau is pacing the perimeter of the lawn, barking whenever
we draw near in an attempt to pet him. I put my backpack on
the table and feel around until I find a giant plastic brick. I pull
out the satellite phone's long antenna, staring for a minute at its
big rubber buttons, then seek the page in my journal where I've
recorded the number for our guide in Sepon, Mr. Bouk, and dial.
No luck.

I try again, feeling my hangover in my temples. And again.

Five tries later, I catch a satellite, and static gives way to our
guide's voice... or rather a string of consonants bleeped by more
static.

"Mr. Bouk?"

"Hello... Who? ...Huh? ...Phone is bad! Bad!"

"Mr. Bouk, it's Jessica Rotondi, your client for Sepon tomorrow."

"...Jessica ...phone not working..."

"Can you hear me now?" I pace the yard, Beau at my heels.
"Now?"

There is a garbled voice as my signal dips out.

"...get Lao phone!"

Click.

"I will email you!" I yell, hoping he heard me before the signal was lost.

I stand in the yard, blinking at the "top-of-the-line" satellite phone in my hands. The one friends and family said would keep me safe when we went off the grid tomorrow. The one with the "panic" button that would supposedly give out my GPS location in case of emergency. The one the phone company touted as usable in mountains and deserts alike. Here, in this gated yard in a capital city, it is already useless. I consider punting it across the yard or giving it to Beau as a chew toy. Liz watches my face drop. She's heard everything.

"He thinks we need a new phone." I roll my eyes.

Liz looks down at the patchy grass beneath the porch before speaking: "You know, I think it's not a bad idea to get the cell phone. What if you need to do follow-up interviews? What if you have to arrange to meet a source?"

My stomach rumbles as I think about my bank account. I stare at the chunk of plastic that cost me close to $350 just to rent lying still on the table and hear again the awful static blocking my guide's voice. I concede her point: we *do* need a second phone.

"We'll need more cash, too," Liz says.

I start to protest: on top of the satellite phone expense, I've closely budgeted the $240 each for our guides, in American twenties in an envelope that hasn't left my body the entire trip. We have $100 worth of Lao kip left, with revolutionary leader Kaysone Phomvihane's face on each orange-and-tan bill. When the money changer handed me the thick pile of rainbow bills at the airport, I thought of the famous photograph of a German woman lighting her stove with German marks after World War I; the heat, to her, had more value than the hyperinflated bills.

"Plus, we still need to buy bus tickets," Liz adds.

The only place to buy tickets is at the bus station itself, half an hour outside of town, and my guidebook says that there are few ATMs in Laos outside of the capital. I look ahead and see our single day in Vientiane, previously full of research stops, filling up with errands. I'd planned so vigilantly to take care of everything, and all my plans are crumbling around me. I take a deep breath, considering our options, but Liz is a step ahead of me.

"You know what? Since we have one day and an eight thirty P.M. bus to catch, let's split up; you start your research, Jess, and I'll take care of finding us a phone and grabbing the bus tickets. If you give me your debit card and PIN, I can withdraw cash for both of us."

My mouth hangs open. In the past few days, I've learned more about Liz than I did in four years of college. She sings when she's truly happy—and for strangers if it will make them relaxed or happier to see her silly side. She puts her wet hair up in a twisty towel. She will ask a question she already knows the answer to, doing it to make you feel involved and loved. She knows how to pack a suitcase with every conceivable variety of tank top. She's as selfless as you'd have to be to join a friend on a journey across the globe in search of something that may not exist. And right now, she is the dearest person in the world to me.

Beau barks as we hug and then, shock of shocks, draws near to us. I reach out my hand and he lifts his head to meet it.

There are some things, I'm learning, you just can't plan in advance.

A car beeps, and Beau breaks away to bark at the gate.

"*Saibaidee!* It's Bounmith!"

Liz and I unlock our old iron nemesis from the night before, swinging the gate open with a screech.

"*Saibaidee,* Mr. Bounmith."

"Good morning," he says in English. "Where to?"

"Coffee, please," Liz and I say in unison, laughing.

I pull my Lao phrase book out of my backpack and Liz and I lean over it together in the back seat. I'd studied a bit in New York, but after a week in Thailand, any progress has been wiped from my tired brain.

"Chow sue nang?"

"Kwa see you Jessica..."

Mr. Bounmith coughs, then laughs, correcting me from the driver's seat: *"Jâo seu nyãng?"*(What is your name?)*"Khãwy seu Jessica, khãwy m a tae America. Saibaideebor?"* (My name is Jessica, I'm from America. How are you?)

I repeat it back.

"Good!"

We pull up to a café called Joma, a Lao chain similar to Starbucks, and order cold yogurt parfaits topped with granola and a *pain au chocolat* to split. I realize that the history of a country—like French colonial rule in Laos—can be told in its breakfast food. We hand Mr. Bounmith a pastry and he smiles.

"Khop jai lai lai—thank you."

"Khop jai lai lai," we repeat.

Mr. Bounmith takes us down more streets framed by protective walls hiding homes, accelerating onto a mini-highway baking in the sun. Fast food and a hotel grace one side; he slows at the other and parks before a giant fountain framed by sagging palm trees.

It's only when I open the car door and feel the heat swarm at my face that I realize something is off: the fountain is dry, not a drop in motion. I step nearer and take in the sweeping white-columned porch behind it. Its grand steps are covered in gray ash and small bits of trash that blow in the wind, paint chipping on the banister. Boards sigh beneath me as I approach the open front door. I pause to let my eyes adjust to the dimness of the lobby; it's 10 degrees cooler now that I'm hidden from the sun. A folding table comes into focus, then the outline of a woman.

"Excuse me, is this the Lao National History Museum?" I ask.

"Yes." She nods.

"Khop jai lai lai."

I dash outside to wave Mr. Bounmith and Liz on their way and then back up the stairs and into the coolness of the lobby, my skin prickling from the contrast. The woman at the table gestures to a sign in Lao and repeats the number in English until I get it: I hand over a note equivalent to one U.S. dollar.

The hallway before me is dark and appears endless in both directions. Floating spots dance before my eyes as they finish adjusting from the move from blinding sun to the cool dark of the museum. *Which way?* I try to go to the right and hear footsteps rushing behind me: it's the woman who sold me the ticket. She gestures—*no, no*—and points to a door to my left. I nod in thanks and hear her steps receding as I enter a small room.

I find myself alone with a bizarre assortment of artifacts. A miniature papier-mâché reproduction of the caves in Sam Neua, dyed the same green Dad used for our milk on St. Patrick's Day, sits alongside a massive, ancient stone vessel from the Plain of Jars. It has been uprooted from the field where it sat beside hundreds of its peers for centuries and placed on the floor at the room's center, reaching halfway to the ceiling. I wonder, like many before me, who made it over two thousand years ago and left it in the sun. How it survived the carpet bombings in the '60s and '70s that destroyed so much else around it.

At the other end of the room, I enter a black-and-white stairwell wrapping up to the next landing. The resemblance to an elementary school is uncanny; I half expect my fourth grade teacher to come and collect me at any moment and scold me for wandering alone in the halls. Creaking and worn white steps spiral upward, framed by a dark banister, a window shedding light on the landing. The sign that greets me at the top announces I've reached the "Hallway of Diversity."

Tucked into a space that could have been a broom closet is a poorly lit display of the "native" dress of minority Lao groups, including the Hmong and Lao Theung. Their clothing, drums, and tools are separated from the unified historical narrative winding around the rest of the building.

It was a long history of ethnic differences, of a hierarchy that placed those who dwelled in the lowlands over those who made their home in the mountains, of forced migrations and bitter animosity, which the Vietnamese and Thai exploited for thousands of years. By the time the Americans chose the Hmong of the mountains as allies against the lowland majority, the C.I.A. training and operating out of their villages, ancient cracks were already appearing in the soil that would soon be rocketed by U.S. bombs.

The Hmong were led by Vang Pao, a major general in the Royal Lao Army—the highest rank ever attained by a Hmong at the time. He was approached by the C.I.A. in 1960 to be the chief of its secret army to push back the communist Pathet Lao. Charismatic and prone to pacing while he talked, the always-in-motion Vang Pao was praised by American officials and his followers alike for fighting alongside his army in battle. But leading guerrilla forces had its costs: the general also flew out bricks of opium on American planes and even set up a heroin laboratory at his base in Long Cheng to help finance the secret war.

After the fall of Vientiane to communist forces, Vang Pao, along with tens of thousands of his loyal Hmong followers, sought refuge in the United States. My grandparents drove out to his ranch in Montana in October 1986, hoping to speak with him about any Americans who may have been left behind. His son had answered the door, saying that his father would return in four or five days and they could make an appointment. The meeting never took place, and on December 8, 1981, my grandmother wrote a letter to the general that alternates between electric anger and pleading:

> Dear General Vang Pao,
> Today I am sad for me and angry and disappointed with you! My son is missing in action near Sepon, Laos... and today is his birthday. He is 34.

My heart stops when I think of my grandmother at her typewriter on her firstborn son's birthday, wanting this general to understand her pain.

> Your son said that when your people regained
> control of your country that American POWs would
> be released. In your opinion can these men hold on
> that long? Can you tell me anything of the treatment
> and condition of American POWs?

She had been holding on to hope for nine years, always wondering if her son could hold on just a little longer, too.

When I asked Francois Vang, Vang Pao's eldest child, if he was the son who spoke to my grandparents that day, he told me it was likely one of his twenty-five siblings.[1] Francois was raised and educated in France during much of the conflict, though he admitted he'd visited his father at his bustling headquarters in Long Cheng, where the sound of airplanes landing and taking off was a constant hum.

Vang was reserved but firm when I asked him about what his father did in the war: "What else could he have done?" he told me. "It was a special time and, from what I know, he did not really want to do that kind of job. It was his responsibility. He was a very ordinary man. I'm sure that he, like anybody else, made some mistakes. A lot of people lie. He knows that. I know that, too." His father commanded an army of thirty-nine thousand guerrilla fighters, thirty-five thousand of whom would die in battle. And according to Vang, his father never spoke to his son about the war:

"Because it was a secret war there were a lot of things that were not supposed to happen. I don't know what happened exactly. War is ugly. You have to do what you have to do to survive. It's them or you. It's not like conventional war where there is a way to treat your enemy, treat your prisoners. It's a secret war...

"I think there is not that much you can gain from talking about all this. There is a lot of bad things happening involving your people, their people, that involve too many people. It's better to let it go and let people live their life."

---

[1] Polygamy was a common practice in Hmong culture. Vang Pao had five wives, four of whom he had to divorce when he moved to the United States.

His voice had changed, and our call ended abruptly. I didn't want to push him any further, talk about all the things I had read, all the questions I had prepared about his father, who was "like the earth and the sky," according to a fellow refugee. Who told the United States that North Vietnam dictated that any prisoners captured by the Pathet Lao had to be turned over to North Vietnam. Who claimed, as late as 1976, that eight to ten American pilots were still captives of the North Vietnamese and being forced to defuse unexploded ordnance across Laos. Who, in 2009 at the age of seventy-nine, was acquitted of charges that he and his associates tried to buy $10 million in weapons from an undercover agent in an attempt to overthrow the communist Lao government he'd spent his career fighting.

Vang Pao's face is not in the Lao National History Museum.

Through a doorway to my right, larger-than-life busts of Ho Chi Minh and Comrade Khamseng Sivilay, "first Communist of Laos," hover over a wood-and-iron shackle with the caption: "French colonialists used to capture Lao people." "American imperialist" guns gather dust on an open wooden platform; there is no glass between the cobwebbed triggers and me. Photos of men and women marching in the streets with AMERICANS, GO HOME signs and burning effigies of Kissinger are placed at eye level. It's hard not to compare them with the photographs I've seen of Vietnam War protests on college campuses back home, students in sweaters with their fists in the air, mouths frozen mid-shout.

As I move down the wall, I am awed by the black-and-white photos of hundred-person-strong meetings in caves and of a class of twenty students sitting at desks under dripping stones, a classroom carved into the rock. I hear the voices of the veterans I've interviewed, the stories and rumors of underground caves and tunnels in Vietnam and Laos, photographed here in the bright flash of a camera brought in so that their children's children could see the strength of the resistance.

The next room is centered around a glass case dedicated to the revolutionary leader of the Pathet Lao and first prime minister of the Lao People's Democratic Republic, the same man memorialized on the bills I withdrew en masse at the airport. It contains "the gun used by Comrade Kaysone Phomvihane to protect himself during the fighting against the U.S. imperialists," alongside "the briefcase for Comrade Kaysone Phomvihane's documents during the fighting against U.S. imperialists," "Kaysone Phomvihane's bag used during the fighting against the U.S. imperialists" (you get the picture), his teakettle, and even a sort of biceps curl contraption.

The most arresting objects are the grainy photos of headless Lao in the bush, victims of American bombs. In one photo, a child bomb survivor stares defiantly into the camera, the remains of his limbs splayed on the chair someone has propped him on, while in an adjacent image, corpses covered in blankets lie on stretchers before a helicopter, the grass twisting from the force of the blades.

More weapons stretch across the base of the photo-covered walls: "This [medium]-sized machine gun used by the militia in Lakhiene [village], Sam Neua district, Houaphanh [province,] had shot down an F4H plane." Nearby is a photo of a bombed-out temple, a Buddha broken into shards.

By far the most striking image of all captures a young man beating his chest with one fist and holding a rifle in the other. One leg is raised as if to step on the mangled, smoking corpse of a plane in the foreground. Two young girls giggle and raise their arms behind him. The photo is captioned: "U.S. imperialist 10 fighter bomber 105 D shot down on 11 May 1965 by a militia man of Phang district, Xieng Khouang province named Thit Chantho twenty-six years old using a rifle."

Surrounded by these photos, it is hard not to think about Jack's chances of survival if he made it out of that plane alive. In all of my grandparents' papers, every document showed their unwavering faith—except for one. It is a recording of a phone call my grandmother made on her own on April 6, 1973, the conversation noted by an airman working at the USAF Missing Persons Branch:

Mrs. Pearce (mother) called in tears to ask if the rumors she had heard about men being killed as soon as they reached the ground in Laos are true. I stated that we had no information that could either confirm or deny these rumors—most of the rumors of Laos are a result of having very little information and therefore news—men jump to different conclusions.

I wonder if she waited until my grandfather was out of the house to make the call, if doubt was something she was able to express to her husband.

I turn away from the photos of smoking planes and walk more quickly through the remaining rooms, stuffed mainly with political manifestos and photos of men shaking hands in ceremonial dress. I need to get out of the maze of exhibits, escape the dusty air pressing against my lungs. *Breathe.* I descend a set of stairs wound like the first and come upon a final dark room.

To my left, what looks like a dismembered doll becomes, as I draw near, a child's prosthetic limb bent at the knee. In the display case opposite is a series of American bomblets lit from below, one of which appears to be inscribed with English letters. I draw closer and lean over the glass, catching a glimpse of my face before I make out the words: FACE TOWARD ENEMY.

The walls of dense photos end abruptly, butting up against a souvenir shop with cheap cotton scarves and carved elephants, the effect disorienting. There is no one behind the counter, no other tourists whom I've encountered in the museum. The air smells like stale paper and something else I can't name.

I start to jog down the hall, following signs for the exit. I push against a white door and burst into the blinding light of the porch that winds around the museum, shading my eyes to scan the road. No sign of Liz or Mr. Bounmith. The heat of midday gathers around me, so dry and persistent it's like a physical force. I want—no, need—to talk to someone about what I've just seen.

A dull ticking sound hangs on the edge of my attention. I follow it, my footsteps soft on the porch as I wind my way to the front entrance of the museum and duck inside. When my pupils adjust, I realize the sound is coming from the ticket booth; the woman is folding brochures at her post, the paper edges scratching at the table beneath her fingers. Across from her, a policeman sleeps, his arms folded across his chest. For a few moments, the only sounds are the shuffling of papers and the soft snores of the officer.

"Excuse me." My voice crackles; I haven't spoken to anyone since I bought my ticket from her hours ago.

The woman raises her eyes.

"Is there someone I can talk to about your exhibits? A guide?"

She holds up a finger and disappears, reemerging with a Lao man not much older than me.

"Hello. You have questions about the museum?" His accent is faintly British, his eyes curious.

"Yes, I was wondering... I would love to learn about the history of Laos." My words come out overly formal. I hardly know what to ask.

"Our museum is full of our history. I suggest you start in this room..."

He gestures to the room of jars and papier-mâché dioramas.

I smile as politely as I can. "I'm very interested in more recent history." I point toward the three-dimensional plaster relief map of Laos in the museum's foyer. "Can you tell me about this map?"

We walk over to it together and he points at the Sam Neua caves.

"Between 1954 and 1975, two hundred thousand people lived in these caves, protected by the army."

I slide my notebook out from my back pocket, the barrier of paper always a comfort when conducting interviews, and begin to take notes.

"The Pathet Lao?"

"Viet Cong," he corrects me.

"What can you tell me about here?" I point to Sepon on the map, marked by a big red dot. There are white stars at the center of a snarl of dotted and solid lines.

"Near Route 9. There were many battles there." He is quiet for a bit, suddenly becoming very interested in his shoes.

I remember what Jack's squadron mate Dave Burns said about how the Sixteenth Special Operations Squadron viewed Sepon:

> [Sepon] was the one place in Laos that we did not want to fly into. The village was at a crossroads of three highways leading in from Vietnam: the Mu Gia Pass, the Ban Karai Pass, and the Barthelme Pass. The highways then headed south to the Ho Chi Minh Trail. It was highly defended with all sorts of anti-aircraft guns. Going there was a guarantee of being hit or being shot down, but we had to go into the area all the time except during the full moon.

Jack went during the full moon and never came back. The People's Army of North Vietnam had launched the Easter Offensive the day after Jack's plane was shot down, storming across the demilitarized zone with two hundred tanks to attack the fire support bases of the Army of the Republic of Vietnam and its American ally.

The museum guide is staring at me, and I realize I don't even know his name. I quickly offer mine: "My name is Jessica, what's yours?"

"Khumphet."

"Khumphet?"

"Yes."

"How do you spell that?"

He gestures to my pen and I hand it to him. He carefully writes his name in my notebook, smiles, hands it back to me. I have the urge to tell him everything.

"I am going to Sepon tomorrow. Have you been there?"

"No."

"My uncle was in a plane that was shot down there many years ago. He was missing for many decades."

"I see." Khumphet avoids my eyes and looks at a spot just below my chin.

"My grandfather tried to go there and could not. I'm going tomorrow to learn about the people he was bombing and about what happened there."

He looks up to take in my full face, and for a moment, neither of us moves, the stale air of the museum still around us.

"I'm sorry for your loss."

I want to tell him that I'm sorry about the broken Buddhas and the bombs, the members of his parents' generation who lost their homes, their families, their lives. Before coming to the museum, I dimly thought of how hard it must have been for my grandparents to educate the American public about where Laos was on a map, about how Americans were secretly sent to bomb this neutral country, about how the missing were left behind, their loss never part of the peace agreement.

Now, for the first time, I see the bomb-cratered country divided by war Americans left behind. The museum erected to create a narrative out of the chaos, a monument to their victory against all odds and at such great cost. I want to convey all this and more, but all I can manage to do is stand there as we blink at each other under the battle map in a dusty museum.

12 / The Trial

I had three sons overseas during the Vietnam era—one Air Force,
one Navy, and one Marine. Now, I find that my government that
I believed and trusted in is lying to me, and this is a greater blow to
me than the fact of not knowing what happened to my son.
—Ed Pearce

Randolph Air Force Base, Texas • March 27, 1979
Jack missing 6 years, 11 months, and 28 days

*E*d and Rosemary have been driving for over twenty-four
hours straight. Every bump in the highway is torture for
my grandfather; he is suffering from hemorrhoids so strong his
eyes sting with the effort to keep his body against the leather seat.
Behind him in the back seat, stacks of folders from the dining
room table shift and plunge with the RV's every turn. With the
road blurring before him as his bowels burn, Ed steps on the gas
like he is driving toward his son instead of the uniformed jury of
hangmen waiting for him.

Forty-eight hours earlier, he and Rosie had been told to
report to Randolph Air Force Base in Texas for their eldest son's
status review hearing. This is no ordinary court appearance.
For six years, Jack has been listed as "missing in action." Now,
the Air Force is asking Rosemary and Ed to go before a military
judge and jury to determine if Jack should continue to be listed
as missing or declared dead with the passage of time. Eight of
the fourteen crew members on Jack's plane have already been
legally declared dead. A ninth family is embroiled in a lawsuit

challenging the military court's right to declare death without a body of proof—or even a body. My grandparents' right to hope is on trial.

Ed and Rosie knew this day would come and had staved it off before. The first time they were served notice of the hearing, they had filed FOIA requests virtually overnight as a way to delay the proceedings. For months, they'd passed reading glasses, cold bread, and Rosie's hobnail glass butter tray over stacks of documents sent from Washington. Uttered "I'll see you in bed" to each other, then lingered an extra hour or two at the table, unwilling to stop until progress had been made. Together, they'd read and reread declassified eyewitness accounts of the crash from pilots in the air that night. Tracked down Jim Spier—the man I'd talk to forty years later—about the last moments Jack was seen alive. Obtained and enlarged maps of Jack's crash site, as if they could glean history from geography. And it worked, at least for a while. They had bought their son more time.

This last notice let them know their time was up. Rosemary and Ed have hired a lawyer who specializes in representing the families of the missing: David Jayne. Jayne had gotten Jack's fellow crewman Charles Wanzel's case continued without a finding, and in a landscape where 100 percent of previous status review hearings led to a "presumptive finding of death," that was no small thing. He believed in the families.

Rosemary had written to Jayne before the hearing, desperate for a way to stop the clock again:

> My husband's mother has just passed away and it was a shock. My husband has very high blood pressure; he takes medication every day to keep it under control and is under a doctor's care. Also, on the other hand, our one and only daughter is getting married May 19th and we find it very difficult to concentrate on wedding arrangements with this hanging over our heads.

I read this and feel the erratic beating of blood against the walls of my grandfather's grieving heart. I imagine my mother at twenty-six, picking out bridal flowers while her parents pick at stacks of paper about Jack.

In the end, my great-grandmother's passing and Mom's wedding aren't enough to stop the Air Force. My grandparents drive the 1,800 miles from Pennsylvania to Texas, high blood pressure and hemorrhoids and grief be damned, to arrive by nine A.M. on the twenty-seventh. Every word uttered in that courtroom is preserved, typewritten on yellow paper that my mother stuffed into a closet beneath the sealed box of her wedding gown.

I picture my grandparents holding hands as they entered the vastness of the "Taj," the administration building and pride of Randolph Air Force Base, with its 170-foot central tower sparkling Air Force blue and gold in the sun. They have to pass murals commemorating the valor of B-17 bombers like Ed's in World War II and Air Force legends in dress blues before entering the courtroom, where they come face-to-face with a formidable row of Air Force brass. All three of Jack's military-appointed jurors had served in Vietnam. One was even a former prisoner of war who shared Jack's Christian name.

Colonel Jack Tomes flew F-105 aircraft out of Takhli, Thailand, and was shot down on his forty-sixth mission over North Vietnam on July 7, 1966. He was one of the "lucky" ones my family had watched returned to U.S. control as part of Operation Homecoming six long years ago. Of all the jurors, surely it's this Jack who knows the value of hope. Beside him is Colonel Lawrence F. McNeil, an A-1 pilot who flew missions out of Nakhon Phanom Royal Thai Air Force Base from '69 to '70. The third juror, Colonel Henry Viccellio Jr., spent over ten years in Southeast Asia and flew more than 240 armed reconnaissance and rescue missions. If Ed has any chance of winning the day, it is to appeal to these men as fellow soldiers who know what it means to be shot at from the sky.

My grandparents are shown to their seats up front, where the small fan blowing hot air around the courtroom barely reaches them. Streams of sweat are already dampening Ed's collar, the measurements grown wider in the three years since he retired from the Pennsylvania State Police to devote himself full-time to the search for his son.

When the judge calls his name, my grandfather rises and adjusts the thick black frames of his glasses, forcing himself to make eye contact with each officer who has the power to declare his firstborn son dead. He hears his attorney introduce him and finds the words he had rehearsed with Rosie in the car:

"As well as being the parent of Sergeant Pearce, I was also a combat pilot in World War II. I participated in one of the largest air battles ever fought, the Schweinfurt and Regensburg raid of 1973. I was shot down on October the 14th, 1943 and was a prisoner of war until 1975 in Stalag 17. I also—"

The dates of his son's shoot-down and his bleed together. I want to tell him to slow down, to give him an extra hour of sleep, of reassurance, but all I can do is read what happens next.

"1945," Rosie corrects.

"I am sorry, thank you. Since the war, I have spent over thirty years in the Pennsylvania State Police. My wife and I have four sons and a daughter. Three of them served overseas in the Vietnam era." Ed looks at all three men, then continues. "Jack was in the Air Force, Mike spent three years in the Mediterranean in the Navy, and my third son spent a year at Iwakuni, Japan, the First Marine Air Wing. And I would like to say that we are the staunchest supporters of this government, and it is painful for me to be here today in what appears to be not a fact-finding case, but a case to dispose of my son, who is guilty of no crime. I feel that it is almost like a firing squad for an innocent man."

My grandfather pauses to let the accusation hang in the Texas air. The judge tells Ed he is in the wrong stage of the proceeding, that there will be time later.

"I wanted this brought in now because I feel even that the law that a missing man should be heard by his peers and I certainly appreciate the gentlemen here today. But not one of them was a

POW of the Pathet Lao, and my son is missing in the secret war in Laos, not in the Vietnamese War. The secret C.I.A.-run war in Laos," Ed challenges.

By 1979, the public had heard rumblings of Air America flights carrying illegal arms and drugs over the Lao border, but to accuse the C.I.A. of a secret war under the dome of the Taj was a bold stroke.

"There will be an appropriate time," the judge warns.

"Right, I am sorry if I—"

"We're in the challenging phase now."

Attorney Jayne shifts the attention away from Ed—who is veering dangerously out of line—to put the heat on the jurors. He approaches Colonel Jack Tomes. "Do you have any opinion on the possibility of servicemen remaining in Southeast Asia in a prisoner of war status?"

"Yes, I have an opinion," Tomes says.

"What is that opinion, Colonel?"

"I don't believe that there are any over there that are being held against their will."

My grandfather lets out a breath. Jayne asks the same question of Colonel McNeil.

"I would say that I probably don't think that they're there, but I would not rule out the possibility," says Colonel McNeil.

Colonel Viccellio didn't need to be prompted: "I am nearer Colonel McNeil's feelings."

Jayne spins around to the judge, triumphant. "Then I could challenge Colonel Tomes for cause. He has already formed an opinion and he could not render a fair and impartial judgment at this time."

"Does an opinion mean there is no possibility?" Colonel Tomes asks, agitated. "An opinion is an opinion. Is an opinion fact?"

The judge intervenes, asking Colonel Tomes if he feels he can make an objective determination.

"Certainly."

Jayne's challenge is denied, so he launches a new tack. "All of these hearings have resulted in a change of status from missing in action to killed in action," he begins, looking at the three colonels before him. "The President of the United States is the only person that can promote [the jurors] to general officer status and I am saying that that promotion is directly influenced by these gentlemen's efficiency reports. If two of these members voted to have this person remain missing in action, it would be noted at all levels of command. These hearings are monitored at all levels and they know that, and I know it, and you know it. How many times in your life do you get to reach for a star?"

The three colonels shift uncomfortably in their uniforms. A ten-minute recess is called. My grandparents are losing these men, if they ever had a chance of winning them over at all.

When the ten minutes are up, the judge returns to deny the challenge. Jayne calls on Ed to speak, and my grandfather rises from his chair as if he could separate the part of his heart that makes him a father from the part that he used when on patrol, the two halves batting around in his chest.

"In our investigation, we've had a photo of the crash site furnished by the Air Force," Ed begins.

Oh, that picture, glossy in his hands. The plane's wing rising up from the jungle like the stiffening body of a broken bird.

"We took that photo to the Marietta, Georgia, plant where the Lockheed AC-130s are built and we talked to a structural engineer. He came out and identified the section of the wing as the wing from an AC-130. He said the wing tip had been sheared off and did not appear to be hit by a SAM. He said that would indicate that *the plane was more or less gliding or declining into the jungle, rather than tumbling or crashing in a dive or a head-on.*"

Ed feels the pull of the parachute that held him up at twenty-two in his ribs, the ground coming up at all angles. The structural engineer's interpretation, he tells the jury, matches the account of the plane crash in the "Rallier's Report" that my grandmother uncovered at the National League of POW/MIA Families convention in '76—the one that went on to say nine men were rescued from the wreckage. I read his argument decades later and sit in awe of the man who never made it past high school standing up to colonels.

"The Executive Branch put the Department of Defense into such a position where it *deliberately and intentionally had to falsify information to the next of kin,*" Grandpa Ed continues, quoting *The House Select Committee Report on Missing Persons in Southeast Asia.* It's as haunting to him now as it was when it was first published in 1976. It brings back anger at the Air Force major who showed up on his doorstep, telling him to keep information about Jack's shoot-down to his immediate family. At Rosie having to fight men in uniform to get the "Rallier's Report" copied and placed in her son's file.

"I have a government that I served for 34 years under oath to lay down my life. Now, I find that my government that I believed and trusted in is lying to me and this is a greater blow to me than the fact of not knowing what happened to my son."

The white-haired World War II veteran and former prisoner of war stands before men young enough to have served with his missing child.

"I could accept his death if there are facts to back it up. I am very proud of him. I know that he felt that he had to do this. He didn't have to go back for his second mission. He went back and volunteered, because he believed in what he was told by President Nixon that if we contained the Communists in Southeast Asia, we'd make the world free and safe for democracy. Now, this same commander in chief, President Nixon, in company with Congressman Ford, traveled to China in February of 1972, a month before my son's plane was shot down."

Nixon's trip to China had been all over the news, earning a certain *New York Times* journalist a Pulitzer. But it pissed my grandfather off, and he was about to let these men know it.

"Now, my son was told to go and fight the Communists and the Chinese were an ally to these Communists and the president, being a military man, the commander in chief, I realize that he is also the president, but he was in China—what would you call it—collaborating with the enemy? Is that treason?"

He has lost them, but he doesn't care. The anger balloons inside him. *Let them hear it and think what they want.*

The judge interrupts: "Mr. Pearce, I think you are going to have to get back on the subject matter at hand."

"I am on the subject matter," my grandfather growls. "I want to tell you right now. I want to tell you right now that when the president went to China—"

The veins in Ed's neck rise with his pulse, his jaw clenching and unclenching. My grandmother's plea to the board rings in my ears: *My husband has very high blood pressure; he takes medication every day to keep it under control.*

"—he was directly responsible for this incident that we are here for today, the shooting down of an AC-130 a month later. General Lavelle of the Air Force issued an order that there will be no air activity above the DMZ while the President is on that trip to China. His rationale at the time was that if he didn't send out limited air raids, they would sneak SAM missiles down the Ho Chi Minh Trail south of the DMZ and our planes would be vulnerable to them. Our plane was the first AC-130 lost in two years," Ed says. And it was lost to a SAM missile launched along the Ho Chi Minh Trail.

Nobody will meet Ed's eyes. My grandfather looks from man to man, daring them to contradict him.

"It is to the government's benefit to wipe the slate clean and sweep the information—sweep this POW/MIA issue under the rug and resume normal relations to get the trade and everything going. Now to do this, President Carter needs a goat, he needs a triggerman, he needs a hatchet man, and you men of the board here today are the ones that he is gonna base his—the Secretary of the Air Force will base his opinion on that. 'The board thoroughly investigated this and found the recommendation of the board to be a presumptive finding of death.' I am no fortuneteller. I don't have a crystal ball, but I know that is what is going to happen. Now, if the men [are] already dead, your conscience will be clear and it is no crime. If the men aren't dead, then I want to tell you as a friend and maybe a father—I don't know if I am old enough to be half you guys' father or not—but I would say that when you are awake in the daylight, in this room, and we are looking at each other we're all men and when you're alone at night in the dark and when you're thinking and it's just you and God there, you're gonna have a conscience battle."

The walls of Stalag 17 gave Grandpa Ed a lot of time to think. He lets himself return to a period in his life he rarely permits himself to access.

"I know that when a man is held in a prison—and I have had the experience—your stomach shrinks, you lose weight; you have no cholesterol problem, no heart attack. A man can live. My son was in excellent physical condition. From the time they were children, we didn't have money, so we did a lot of camping, hunting, and fishing. I know my son could survive."

Jack had eaten the eyeball of a rabbit in Air Force survival school in Fairchild, Washington. He and the other airmen had been held captive for three days by veterans from the Korean War and World War II before being let loose to survive in the woods with a parachute, a pocket knife, a potato, and an onion, trapping wild game and living off the land. I think of the photos of my uncles and Mom as kids with homemade fishing poles on display in my grandparents' bedroom, of Mom's stories of camping with her siblings and my grandmother baking bread over campfires.

Ed continues, his voice breaking: "You just don't die when you feel like it. When you are in prison, you live one day at a time and you adjust. Dying is a thing that the Lord decides."

The room is constricting around Ed's throat; his wife is looking at him strangely.

"Mr. Pearce, would it assist you if we let Mrs. Pearce talk for a little bit?" Jayne asks.

Rosie puts her hand on Ed's shoulder, his heart rate rising to her palm. He forces himself to sit as she rises. When I read the transcript of what happens next, I second-guess how well I knew my grandmother, a woman who worked as a bagger at a grocery store and left lipstick on the cheeks of her grandkids.

"At the risk of calling this an adversary meeting, I would like to know this: Why doesn't the Air Force have a civilian judge as counsel with no ties to the military? Speaking from an MIA family viewpoint, I think that the family itself would feel better if there was a civilian..."

The judge takes the bait: "Well, of course, it is a matter of degree of—"

"Integrity, I suppose," my grandmother finishes.

Ed tries not to smile, fails.

"I hope that you can have some confidence in my integrity," the judge says. "I do not feel in any sense that there is anybody, Secretary's Office or General Counsel's Office, or any place else that is going to second guess what I do or—"

"Or advise you what to do?" I imagine my grandmother's right eyebrow rising three-quarters of an inch, like it did when she caught us sneaking food off plates before dinner, daring us to deny we'd been caught.

"Or advise me what to do. I recognize your point. I am in uniform. I am in the same uniform that these men wear."

"Thank you." My grandmother turns to the jury. "Now, I would like to know if any of you gentlemen are acquainted with an AC-130? Have you ever flown in one?"

"I never have," Colonel McNeil says.

"I have."

Rosemary turns to Colonel Viccellio, intrigued. "You have. The AC-130?"

"Mm-hmm."

"And Mr. Tomes? Colonel Tomes, is it? I am sorry."

My grandfather smiles again.

"No, I have never flown on an AC-130. Passenger on a 130."

"So you have never flown in one." I can't help but note that the stenographer has recorded this as a statement, not a question.

Rosie continues: "The F-4 escort [plane] of Spectre 13 saw a SAM come off the ground and hit Spectre 13 at approximately

0300 hours. And at 0350 hours, a Nail FAC [plane] covering the crash site said it did not observe any parachutes. My question is, was the plane unobserved for a full hour, and how could anybody possibly expect to see a parachute in the air after an hour?"

"I don't think he could have seen any parachutes anyway because it was night," Colonel McNeil responds.

Rosemary continues, triumphant: "And now in the records as the 5th of April, '72, it says two F-4 escorts and Spectre 10 heard survival radio beeper transmissions several minutes after Spectre 13 was seen to crash. The beepers came from the area of the crash site, though no voice contact could be established. Although other aircraft in the area saw no parachutes, *it is possible for some of the crewmembers of Spectre 13 to have bailed out.*"

In the copy I later hold in my hands, my grandmother has underlined a phrase from that report: "<u>the possibility of their survival still exists</u>," the pencil line nearly ripping through the paper.

My grandfather speaks: "I am striving for the truth. I know that we'll accept the truth whatever it is... but we want the evidence to not be tampered with, not altered, and be considered. I think a lot of evidence was altered here not necessarily by the Air Force, but by the C.I.A. and the D.I.A., the same people who were forced to issue false statements to the next of kin originally."

I think of the black bars that stripe the declassified reports my grandparents collected, the contradictions they'd spent six years trying to unravel.

"I have a statement from Captain Howard Rowland," Rosemary adds. "'Shortly after the explosion, we heard a distress beeper on guard frequency. As we were leaving our working area, we obtained approximate UHF DF positions on the beeper. The beeper appeared to be coming from the general area of the crash site. We were directed by Moonbeam to area 6B. We worked this area until forced to retire by daylight. While working this area, we heard a faint beeper intermittently.'

"'*All night*' it said in the original, I don't have that one here, but it—'*we heard a faint beeper intermittently all through the night.*' Well, this would lend credence to the fact that there were men on the ground."

Rosemary pauses to look at the three colonels. Lingers on Jack Tomes.

"An AC-130 pilot confirmed that so many beepers were heard that the two pilots of an accompanying aircraft who did the listening were unable to count them. He said that the two pilots who originally reported the beepers were ignored and their reports hushed up. However, they made such a stink about the cover-up that the reports became common knowledge. He said if those pilots had not pushed, that report would not have been acknowledged at all."

Over the past four hours, my grandparents have accused the C.I.A. of a secret war, of covering up facts, and of silencing airmen about the survival of their peers in open court. The judge is growing impatient.

Rosemary raises her voice: "In no country in Indochina has there been any search of the crash areas, and I think that this would lend a lot of credence to the Air Force's presumptions. It is important that the family know what happened to their man."

My grandfather backs her up: "We were assured by President Nixon to play it low-key so that Hanoi would release the POWs that they admitted holding and we would work on the MIA situation later. Then, when the last POW stepped off the plane"— Ed looks at Colonel Tomes—"he stated, 'I have ended the longest war in U.S. history and brought all of our POWs home with honor.' There were still 80 men listed as POW when he was making that statement," my grandfather says. "My son as well as the other prisoners are being just abandoned."

My grandparents speak as one.

"Over 500 in Laos—"

"Over 500 in Laos—"

"One at a time," the judge responds.

"Oh, I am sorry." Ed says. He locks eyes with Rosemary.

The judge rises to announce the jurors will deliberate in closed session, says that their findings will be based on majority vote.

Ed takes in his wife's face, her skin flushed the way their daughter's—and, later, mine—gets when she's upset, red capillaries bursting under blue eyes. She has spent four hours and ten minutes defending her son before a roomful of men after more than six years of waiting for news.

When the jury returns thirty minutes later, it is Colonel Jack Tomes who reads the verdict aloud, sending shock waves of anger into my grandfather's blood from which he'll never recover:

"After evaluating all of the evidence placed before it by the United States Air Force and the Next of Kin, the panel finds that on the weight of credible evidence Senior Master Sergeant Edwin J. Pearce, FR192-38-7175, can reasonably be presumed to be dead. The panel recommends that the status of Senior Master Sergeant Edwin J. Pearce, FR192-38-7175, be changed under 37 US Code 555 or 556 from missing in action to killed in action."

Jack Pearce had been missing for six years, eleven months, and twenty-eight days. And now, in this Texas courtroom, the U.S. government has decided he is dead.

Part II / *Blood*

13 / COPE

If the Lord says, "You're dead," I'd advise you to lay down. But if the
government says, "You're dead," I'd think twice about it.
—Ed Pearce

Vientiane, Laos · November 21, 2013 · Mom gone 4 years, 23 days

If you take a right at the hospital off Khou Vieng Road, you'll
come across a tiny white building with brown lettering on its
roof. If you look closer, you'll see the letters are made from wooden
prosthetic hands, feet, arms, and legs that spell "COPE."

When I told friends I was heading for Laos, few knew where
to find it on a map. Fewer still were able to identify it as the most
heavily bombed country in the world. American forces dropped
270 million cluster bombs over Laos between 1964 and 1973, and
it's estimated that 80 million still lie buried beneath the soil. About
fifty people a year still die from unexpectedly setting them off—40
percent of them children.

The Cooperative Orthotic and Prosthetic Enterprise, better
known by its eerily appropriate acronym of COPE, was founded
in 1997 to aid survivors of explosions from bombs left in Laos
after the secret war. I've come here to understand how the bombs
dropped from my uncle's plane and the planes of other Americans
are still impacting the descendants of the families my grandfather
walked among in 1973.

Mr. Bounmith drops us off by the entrance and says he'll wait
in the car.

"Jess, look." Liz grabs my arm and nods to our left.

*A mother and child statue made of bomb fragments
stands outside the COPE Visitor Centre.*

I look up at a life-sized sculpture standing just beside the main door. It depicts a mother holding her child's hand as they run away from something in the sky. One of her arms is raised over her head, fingers frantic and stretched in protection. Both figures are made from bomb fragments left to rust in the sun.

The entrance to the museum is via a small, unmanned gift shop. Liz and I walk past racks of T-shirts featuring an unlicensed Hello Kitty leaning on crutches. Stuffed teddy bears and elephants sized for small hands are piled nearby.

"Saibaidee!"

A twentysomething man emerges from a back storeroom and welcomes us, gesturing toward the doorway behind him. We hand him the bills we'd brought as donations and enter the main room of the museum, where we are greeted by a mobile of metal balls dangling from the hangar-like ceiling—unexploded cluster bombs. The rusted orbs are frozen in permanent fall toward the bottom half of a hollowed-out bomb, collecting them like a bowl of raindrops at our feet. To our right, an animated video is displayed on an endless loop. In it, a young brother and sister play together, then begin to sow their parents' fields. A few minutes in, we see a close-up of the girl digging. Then there's light. An explosion. Shadows fly over the fields and resolve themselves into the shape of American planes. In English, the film announces, "Laos is the most heavily bombed country in the world..."

I watch the video loop through at least twice, seeing Jack's AC-130 in the cartoon shadows that cross over the animated mountains and fields. Every time, the brother runs toward the blast and the shadow of the planes, arriving at his sister too late. A rustling behind me makes me jump. In a corner to our left, a man crouches behind an expensive-looking camera and tripod arranged on the floor. He sees me staring and straightens up.

"Sorry if I scared you." His accent is American as he laughs at me. He puts out his hand and introduces himself. "Jon."

"I'm Jessica." I gesture behind me. "And this is Liz."

I nearly step on what he's photographing as I go to shake his hand; his arm guides me away just in time. The item I almost tripped over, he explains, is a piece of "unexploded ordnance" recently unearthed from a nearby field. An unexploded bomb.

An unexploded bomb that I almost walked right on top of.

As I recover from the shock, he asks where we're from, and I explain that we're visiting from New York. My eyes stay on the rusting specimen at our feet.

"That's a hike from Laos," Jon says.

It's my turn to laugh, the sound uncomfortable in a room full of weapons.

He tells us he used to be a photographer in New York: "Street scenes. People. Now, I photograph this." He gestures to the room around us. He's been photographing the Doctors Without Borders team in Laos and is at COPE to document the bombs that villagers are still pulling up from the earth. The people of rural Laos live in constant fear of setting off these remnants from the war, he explains, even decades after the Americans left. "What brings you here?"

"She's here to research her family," Liz says proudly, her arm on my shoulder.

Jon looks at me, then back to Liz.

"My uncle was in the Air Force," I tell him, my gaze still on the bomb on the floor. "His plane was shot down over Sepon back in 1972."

"Sepon." The man nods. "Sure. I know a couple that goes to Sepon every year with We Help War Victims. It's a hike from Vientiane. The roads can be impassable."

"I hadn't heard that," I say noncommittally, relieved that he hadn't asked what Jack was doing in Sepon. *Impassable roads. Will the van we hired be able to take us where we need to go?*

"We're heading there on the overnight bus in a few hours," Liz replies.

Jon glances from blond woman to blond woman. "The two of you on the night bus, alone?"

"Is there a better way to get there?" I think back to the nights of researching this trip in Brooklyn, typing out our itinerary for Liz on Google Docs: "Cheapest option, only $18! VIP bus even has A/C (exclamation point!)!"

The man shakes his head and chuckles. "You have to work with what you've got in Laos."

We exchange email addresses on shreds of paper from my notebook and leave him to his work. I watch from behind an exhibit plaque as he re-crouches on the cement floor to check the camera shutter, his eyes inches away from the bomb. I follow Liz up the wooden steps of a traditional Lao hut that has been rebuilt inside the museum. From a small viewing platform, we can look down through a hole cut into the boards beneath our feet. It reveals a dirt floor with a faux cooking fire. Nearby, two unexploded bombs are shown in the locations where real bombs detonated on a mother and child who lived in the hut on which our surroundings are based. Signs tell us that cooking fires lit in Lao homes like this one often heat the soil beneath them, setting off buried bombs and killing or maiming the person who had the misfortune to cook her supper over a former war zone.

Also on display are ladles, spoons, and forks in odd shapes made by locals—all from unexploded bombs. I try to wrap my head around a bomb falling from a U.S. plane and being dug up for rebirth as a spoon by the people it was supposed to kill. Then again, my grandfather carried his spoon from Stalag 17 across continents as a message to his future children.

Looking away, I draw near the framed children's drawings mounted on the right wall of the room. As I lean closer, I see black triangles signifying huts sprouting scribbled flames and smoke. Thick lines of red consume stick figures caught in midmotion as planes circle the crayon skies overhead. Below each piece is the child artist's description of what his or her drawing captures:

> These three were worried about their belongings in
> the house. If everything burned, what were they to

do to care for their future lives, to have rice to put in their stomachs? These three, mother and her two sons, ran out of the mouth of the cave. Their goal was to go to their burning home and retrieve some of their belongings to have for their future lives. But their fate was ended. Just then a bomb from the airplanes hit them. That bomb was a very big bomb. They were careful, but the fragments struck them. All three people in this one family lost their lives due to the necessities of war. This is the real fruit of war! That people die for no reason and no result!

The next part is almost too hard to read: "There were people who died in the holes. There were many people who couldn't get out. All that could be seen were heads, and legs, and hands only. Then there was a man who went to dig them out because his child and wife were buried inside."

The walls of the hut feel too narrow; I need to get out. I descend the steps so quickly I nearly stub my toe on them, looking up just in time to find myself once again in the open hangar-style room but with a terrifying twist: a forest of limbs in wood and plastic dangles above my head. I turn to Liz behind me, and her neck is craned up, too, her face melted in horror.

The limbs hang from the high ceiling by wires of varying lengths, legs swaying in the draft. Some hang so low the bare, unattached feet looked as if they just jumped off the floor on their own; I half expect them to come clattering down at any moment. We walk past child-sized legs and thick adult limbs, feet made from wooden shoehorns and sophisticated, flesh-colored toes suspended at eye level.

Something my uncle Kim told me about the AC-130 planes sticks in my skull as I stare at a sock stretched over a prosthetic foot: "A friend I worked with, a welder, remembers calling out for help in 'Nam and giving coordinates to a Spectre, the type of plane Jack was in. The plane opened fire on everything around them,

Prosthetic limbs dangling from the ceiling of the COPE Visitor Centre.

and after the firing ceased, everything—trees, bushes, people—were dead. 'You could stand up and walk around like it was a park,' he said."

At the edge of the leg forest is a small wooden table with three prosthetic hands and hairbrushes labeled THE TOOLS OF THE TRADE. Next to it, a smaller sign indicates we are to sit and touch the objects on top of an adjacent table. I hesitate briefly before placing my hands in the "mirror box," a wooden box with a central, mirrored partition separating my right hand from my left.

"Placing the arm into the box and looking into the mirror fools the brain into thinking that the reflection is the missing arm and so moving the arm, massaging or scratching the place where the itch is perceived can help."

I wiggle my left thumb, watching its reflection in the mirror, and then my invisible right. When I still my left hand, the mirror image of my still fingers is chilling. "Phantom pain," the visitor card explains. I recoil from the mirrored box, pulling my fingers back and touching them to make sure they are still there. It's not until my chair scrapes back that I realize I've been holding my breath.

I let the air out and approach the center of the room, where a freestanding chalkboard—the kind you'd find at the front of a classroom—acts as a divider between exhibits. A pair of small crutches leans against the board. Five photos of children are framed at its center, each of them missing at least one limb. The chalkboard is covered in inspirational words written in English in every shade of the rainbow: "Hope" in blue. "Compassion" in peach. Across the top of the board, chalk letters are pressed hard into the wooden frame: "IMPOSSIBLE IS NOTHING."

I hear my mother at the Lao embassy in 1975: *I have reason to believe that my brother may still be alive through concrete evidence... Unfortunately, it has been impossible to access the crash site since that date, so further information has not been garnered...* The Air Force to my grandparents in 1982: *The Pearces say they... have been told remains are almost impossible to recover due to the rugged terrain and the climate.*

The photographer's warning about the impassable roads ahead rings in my ears. The weight of the dangling limbs above seems to press in on all sides until I feel physically ill.

"Liz, I'm going to get some air," I say. "I'll meet you outside."

She is putting her hands in the mirrored box; I watch her face change as she tries to wiggle her fingers, only to see the still reflection of an unmoving hand. Liz looks from the mirror to my face. "I'm coming with you."

Together, we wind our way through the limb forest to take refuge in the solar glare of the parking lot and Mr. Bounmith's waiting car. If he sees the statue of mother and child made of bombs as we drive past it, he doesn't react to it. Perhaps it's something you become accustomed to.

As we exit the parking lot, the car fills with an uncomfortable silence. Liz finally punctures it: "Mr. Bounmith, would you like to join us for lunch?" We are driving past the hospital, where there's a line of people holding roses, balloons, and oversized teddy bears as they wait to visit loved ones.

"Oh, I couldn't," he says.

"Please. You've been so good to us. We'd like to thank you," Liz insists.

He hesitates. "I'm not sure you'll like Lao food."

"We like what you like. Let's go to a place that suits you," I tell him.

"Do you like soup?" he finally asks.

It's at least 90 degrees outside, and soup sounds terrible. Liz and I exchange a look. "Soup sounds great!"

Twenty minutes later, Liz and I sit across from Mr. Bounmith, a sticky table shrink-wrapped in Coca-Cola branding between us. A fan blows over the three of us, bringing the smells of lemongrass and sriracha from the other tables.

From my side of the bench, I can see through to the front of the restaurant. It opens out onto the street, the sound of motorcycles and the yells of street vendors mixing with the fragrances emanating from the proprietor's big pot. She cooks by the open door, and locals are gathering outside to pick up lunch.

Liz asks Mr. Bounmith about his family. He has a wife and two kids, a son and daughter both under the age of ten. His daughter wants to be a doctor.

"I live a ways away from Mr. Tan. I leave before my children go to school."

I think of his early arrival this morning, of the hours he spent away from his family as he watched us eat dinner the night before, and feel guilty.

"You have a long ride ahead of you tonight," Mr. Bounmith says, seeing my face and changing the subject. "When do you arrive in Sepon?"

"Tomorrow morning, around six A.M. It's an overnight bus," I explain.

"I see," he says, looking unsure. "The roads are not easy. And forgive me, but how do you plan to speak to the people of Sepon? Do you have friends there?"

"Through our translator," I say.

"Have you met him before?"

"No."

Mr. Bounmith looks down at his lap. "They may not want to talk to you. Americans, Lao... it is hard."

"Do you think you could write a note for us to give to people in Sepon? To tell them that they can trust us?" Liz asks.

He stares at Liz for a minute, then drops his eyes to the table. "Yes. Yes, I can do that."

I move to get my notepad and pen from my backpack.

"Not now," he says as the waiter brings us heaping bowls of broth and noodles. "In the car."

The conversation is reduced to slurps, and Mr. Bounmith is right: the pho is delicious. The aroma of basil and garlic rises up and steams my very pores.

Once we're back in the car, I tear away a tiny page of my notebook and hand it to him.

"What do you want it to say?" Mr. Bounmith asks.

How to even start? I wonder. There's so much I want to know. "Hello. My name is Jessica, from the USA..."

He looks at me in a way that lets me know that may not be the best opening line.

"What would you start with?" I ask him. "I want to be as polite as possible."

Mr. Bounmith writes for a bit, then reads us what he's written, translating as he goes: "I am so sorry to bother you, but I am wondering if you can help me find out what happened to my uncle. His plane crashed on March 29, 1972, near this village. Can you please help me?"

I hold the note in my hands and smile at him gratefully. "Thank you so much. This means so much to me and my family."

"If you need help or a translation, you call me and put the person on the phone," he says. He gives me his business card. He is younger in his picture, with a tie and collared shirt snug and smart under his chin. I am so appreciative I don't know what to say, so I catch his eye in the rearview mirror and smile.

Patuxai Gate looks even more Parisian in the daylight as we drive past it. We watch women parade under parasols of red and green and white not to weather raindrops, but to protect their pale skin from the Lao sun. I can't help but think of Grandpa Ed strolling among them years ago. I watch the gate grow smaller as we leave it behind. Liz and I have a few more hours before our long-awaited journey to Sepon, and my courage is beginning to shrink along with the view.

Mr. Bounmith motions ahead, and I turn my attention to the golden spire growing larger as we approach it: Pha That Luang, the Buddhist stupa on the cover of virtually every Lao travel guide and plastered on a thousand postcards. My grandfather was here in 1973, his neck bright with sunburn above his short-sleeved polyester shirt. The stupa allegedly contains Buddha's breastbone, buried there in 3 B.C., but my guidebook casts doubt on this assertion, pointing to Khmer origins and a nearby monastery constructed sometime between the eleventh and thirteenth century. Now, as we pull into the trash-filled parking lot surrounding the spire, it looks as if it has lost some of its original sheen.

Mr. Bounmith says he'll wait in the car, and Liz and I walk into the stultifying heat rising up in solid pulses from the pavement. We pass carts hawking key chains and other souvenirs to arrive at the main entrance cut into the wall surrounding the stupa. The tall doorway is covered in cheap orange and gold theater curtains that block the view of the temple until you pay. I am struck by the difference between this religious monument and the open, inviting temples of Thailand. This seems all gaudy, a show of strength. We hand over our kip and pull back the curtain to get a closer look.

The spire's height is impressive, but as I draw nearer, I notice the stupa's gold paint is peeling and its white base is covered in dirt splashed up from some long-ago rain. Stone benches along one side are spattered in drips of marigold wax. Crushed yellow candles and more wax spatter cover the ground beneath them, drying in the sun. We walk around the monument's base in the crunching grass, unsure of what to do next. A set of small platforms with covered shrines radiate from the first level of the graded stupa. Their floors are arrayed with sun-shaped offerings of bananas and marigolds, the painted figures of Buddha draped in fresh flowers. I remove my shoes, the cement steps burning the balls of my feet, and ascend to one of the smaller shrines. I kneel on the woven mat, trying to find the same groundedness I had found in Chiang Mai.

Staring at the faux gold stupa, I realize why I feel so agitated when I look at it: it is the exact color of the burial vault I picked out for Mom.

The day after Mom died, Morgan, Dad, and I had stood in a darkened room in a funeral home, trying to figure out how to pick a casket. Morgan and I walked over to the same one. It was made of dark wood, like the mahogany table Mom loved, with brass handles that matched the ones she'd picked out for her master bathroom. It struck me then, as now, that we were so ill prepared for her death that we were reduced to making burial choices based on our mother's favorite bathroom fixtures.

The casket chosen, all I wanted was to leave the darkness of the funeral home and sleep through the unreality of the next few days. But then the funeral director led us into a second room and explained that there was an outer box we could buy—yes, he actually used the word "box"—to protect our loved one.

"This one here," he'd said, pointing to one painted to look like brass, "is waterproof. It prevents the water from seeping in."

The thought of my mother submerged in groundwater took the very air out of my lungs. "We can't let her get wet," I told Dad. "Please."

As I said it, my sister ran her hands through her spiked hair, recently buzzed for Locks of Love, with a horrified look on her face that said, *I just lost a mother and now my sister's losing it, too.* But Dad was too exhausted to say no.

At the gravesite a few days later, the waterproof box shone in the sun beside the open grave, and the paint that had looked like a colonial brass in the dark room was suddenly a tacky gold.

I hear movement behind me and see two small children removing their sandals to approach the platform, their fists filled with flowers. I descend the steps as the children get on their knees in the shrine, looking back to their parents for guidance.

I find Liz standing on the dry lawn and we head toward the parking lot together, both of us anxious to leave. All around us on the hot pavement, vendors have arranged miniature painted Pha That Luang replicas. Its golden spire adorns commemorative spoons, plates, and magnets. One merchant has placed an array of bright plastic toys at a child's eye level. Liz kneels before it and pulls up a set of plastic cars in faded packaging.

"How do you feel about giving these to the kids in Sepon?" she says. "It would be nice to bring gifts."

I am struck again at how prepared and practical she is, how unprepared and awkward I am in comparison. We buy the cars, and the plastic bag Liz carries them in rustles as a rare breeze floats across the parking lot. I spot another spire, this one horizontal and protruding from what appears to be the head of a giant reclining Buddha. I turn my head to look at Liz.

"Go," she says. "I'm right behind you."

Buddha's giant scale becomes more apparent as we approach. Beneath him is a red and gold base that stretches for hundreds of feet, dwarfing the two mature trees planted on either side of his elegant body. In the open air, the yellow of his giant toes is striking, the pads of each foot embedded with a dharma wheel larger than my face. Up close, the freshness of the paint pops.

From his toes I walk along his legs to his knees, stomach, and shoulders, then up to his calm face and closing eyes. I look at my guidebook, which explains that depicting the Buddha in this reclining pose symbolizes his release from this life, a resting from his final illness. Letting go.

The idea has followed me everywhere here, I think as we climb back into the car.

"Do you like Buddha?" Mr. Bounmith asks from the front seat, his eyes on mine in the rearview mirror. Liz turns to me as well. I wonder if she saw me staring at the giant statue, how much she'd read in my face.

"I love him," I respond. I push thoughts of the people I've lost away and focus on the two people with me in the hot car.

Mr. Bounmith nods. "Well, then may I take you to a place I think you would like?"

We have a few hours remaining before our night bus departs Vientiane for Sepon. Since the moment he wrote that note for me, I've come to trust the man in the driver's seat with all my being.

"Yes, I would like that very much."

"I think you will find it beautiful," Mr. Bounmith says.

When we pull over by a high wall and exit the taxi, I gasp. The temple of Wat Sisaket is rimmed in covered stone walkways, each flanked by two tiers of seated Buddhas draped in orange silk. The light inside is cool and gray, and as I walk slowly among their beautiful, varied faces—noting a chipped nose here, a more recessed brow there—I'm filled with a feeling of impossible calm. There is a break in the terraced walls of Buddhas that jars me: a recessed stairwell covered with iron bars. Behind the bars are rows and rows of shattered Buddhas. A wooden sign posted nearby in English reads: "These broken pieces of the Buddha statues were destroyed by the war. [They] were found underground during excavation in the Vientiane city."

Every single Buddha, even the broken ones, faces the central temple, and when we go inside, I understand why. As my eyes adjust from the bright sky to the spotlights aimed up at the ceiling, I see the stories-tall central Buddha lit from below, his golden body seated in the same meditative cross-legged position as the hundreds of figures facing him from every direction. He is flanked by two standing figures, both with their hands outstretched palm-first to the people below: "Buddha calming the ocean."

Liz and I crane our necks upward, taking it all in. When she turns to leave, I quietly raise my two palms, the mirror image of the Buddhas above me. We stand there, the Buddhas and me, our long fingers reaching toward the sky in the semidark.

At the bus station, Mr. Bounmith vacates the driver's seat to grab our bags. I am hyperaware of his handwriting in the notebook strapped inside my travel wallet, which dangles against my ribs under my sweaty T-shirt. Its corners poke into my skin as I hug him and try not to cry. This quiet man has done so much for us, offered so much help, and shared his city and his language. I overcome the urge to watch him drive away by bending over to consolidate the snacks in my backpack. When I stand up again, he is already gone.

The station around me smells of cigarettes and tightly packed bodies, so Liz and I decide to board the bus as early as possible. The 8:30 VIP night sleeper bus to Savannakhet is so narrow we can't fit down the aisle with our bags, so we leave them under the bus and try again. I take a deep breath and force my body to move straight ahead, arms at my sides, before climbing up a metal ladder like the one in Grandma Rosemary and Grandpa Ed's camper.

Our "seat" is a twin-sized mattress pad positioned three feet from the bus ceiling. It's so small that only one of us can sleep on our back at a time. We stuff our wallets and cash into our underwear and tuck our shirts into our pants. Liz curls up by the window, and I take the aisle spot, my back to the heavyset man readying himself for sleep across from us. I'm grateful all over again that Liz and I are traveling together; single passengers are stuck sharing beds with strangers.

I'm so exhausted I don't hesitate to put my head on the bright pink bus pillow or bring the fleece blanket featuring a cartoon character I don't recognize up to my chin. The last thing I remember before falling asleep is the chill of the air-conditioning, the vibration of the wheels beneath the thin mattress, and the sight of the Big Dipper upside down in the blue-black sky outside the window. It is the farthest away from home I have ever felt.

14 / Politically Depressed

34 years of my life were spent under oath to "lay down my life"
in the service of this country, either as a soldier in WWII or a PA state
policeman upholding the law and I taught my sons to love their country—
What a FOOL—what a wasted life!

—Ed Pearce

VA Hospital · Wilkes-Barre, Pennsylvania · October 3, 1983
Jack missing 11 years, 6 months, and 4 days

*E*d settles into the stiff chair across from Dr. Cupple at the
Wilkes-Barre Veterans Administration Hospital, the chair
barely containing his 6-foot-tall, 204-pound frame. His once dark
blond hair is now completely white and combed over a browned
scalp that's beginning to peek through. His skin is a deep tan from
a summer of hunting in Montana, the color striking against the
chilly blue gray of the shirt Rosie has ironed for him. *To bring out
your eyes*, she'd said.

But it's Grandpa Ed's eyes that betray him. He hasn't slept
through the night in weeks, and it shows. He sits in the exam
room with his hands in his lap, his black dress shoes worrying
the linoleum floor, while he waits for the doctor to begin. As a
former prisoner of war, Ed is eligible for a variety of benefits at the
local VA hospital, including a program called a "Mental Hygiene
Clinic"—as if to say if you could only scrub the folds of your brain
a little harder, you'd be clean; if you can press your dress blues,
you can tidy up your head.

10/3/83

Mental Hygiene Clinic

Reason for request: Sixty-one-year-old male c/o depression, inability to sleep. Former POW. Has son missing in action for eleven years.

Has been "fighting" the government to get the men listed MIA home. He feels they are alive. Was a prisoner of war. Does not feel he is depressed now. Wants to talk @ length about his deep concerns regarding the men he feels are still being held by Vietnam, Laos, Cambodia.

It's my feeling this man's problem is political and not psychiatric. He does not seem to need psychiatric attention, but rather is interested in getting someone to listen to his personal concerns. He has flown to Laos already. He says the only one that can help him is the White House.

Ed had not been part of the parade of uniforms marching past the White House on November 3, 1982, when 150,000 people gathered for the dedication of the Vietnam Veterans War Memorial, the gusts of wind so strong they knocked over coffee cups and gave the majorettes marching alongside former soldiers goose bumps. Jack's name is etched into the black marble on panel 2W, line 122, not far from where Ed once picketed the White House to demand a full accounting of the war missing.

"They built a monument to Vietnam veterans down there in Washington and put our son's name on it. But he is not dead. He is missing in action," Ed tells anyone who will listen. A friend sent him a rubbing of Jack's name, pressing the wax paper against the monument's mirror of black marble until EDWIN J. PEARCE transferred from stone to paper. When Ed opened it, the graphite around the emptiness of the letters came off on his hands. He held on to his son's absence instead of his son.

Ed continues to cling to the eyewitness testimony saying that nine men were rescued and, in May 1983, catches a break: a CBS News crew and American representatives of *Soldier of Fortune* magazine contact JCRC officials to tell them that members of the Lao resistance—a group still attempting to overthrow the communist government from within Laos—have recovered personal effects of downed pilots in the wreckage of an AC-130. One resistance member claims he went into the cockpit and found four or five skeletons before he removed a wedding ring inscribed *Forever Sue*: Curtis Miller's. The information was passed to Sue Miller, whose daughter writes a heartbreaking letter to the chargé d'affaires:

> Dear Mr. Bounkeut,
>
> I am the daughter of Major Curtis Daniel Miller who is missing in action in your country since March 29, 1972... We have been told that four or five bodies were in the cockpit of that aircraft when it was located in April 1983. Could you please find out what has happened to those bodies that were found? I would appreciate it so much if you would return those remains to America. It would be of great comfort to me if I could find out if my father's body is one of those and if you would return it so as he could be buried in his native soil of Texas.

The government knows where the plane is. The cockpit is intact. Four to five bodies—not fourteen—were present. That meant it was possible that nine men could have survived. But Americans can't access the crash site directly; the Lao government is distrustful of letting the same Americans who trained Hmong forces to rise up against it back into the country.

"They'd think maybe we're working for the former Royal Lao people," says Sompatana "Tommy" Phisayavong, a research analyst at the Department of Defense from Vientiane. "Even when

I was at a refugee camp, the resistance, the old regime, was trying to get the country back. They were fighting pockets here and there all the way to the 2000s. It didn't die back in '75."

Tommy's father was a pilot in the Royal Lao Air Force, the same force Rosemary Conway was attempting to get out of the country in 1975. When Tommy was thirteen, representatives of the new Lao government came to the family's door and told his father, "You need to go with us. We're going to send you to reeducation camp just to train you up with the new regime for three months or so. No worries."

"We packed up his bags and sent him on," Tommy tells me. "Three months turned out to be twelve years. He was in that reeducation camp somewhere in northern Laos for twelve years."

Tommy's mother made arrangements for him and his eleven-year-old brother to escape across the Mekong River to Thailand, where they lived in a refugee camp with their aunt until 1979, when they traveled to the United States. "I thought, *I'm never going to see Laos again*," he tells me.

Tommy has since been back to Laos more than a hundred times as part of the JCRC, translating for the archaeologists exhuming remains from the red earth. But in 1984, he is still a teenager in Los Angeles, dreaming of joining the Air Force like his father as he waits for him to come home. The planes he'll one day raise from the ground sit exposed to the sun and elements, guerrilla fighters picking them clean as families wait for news.

5/2/85

Mental Hygiene Clinic

This country has been marking the 10 yr anniversary of the end of the Vietnam War and the fall of Saigon. A lot of attention has been focused on MIAs. Patient has a son who is MIA. Patient appeared on television earlier this week on the local news. He spoke about this and how the U.S. gov't

*is covering up things... Was advised at sometime in the
past that his depression is not a psychiatric problem, but a
political one. He made jest of this. It seems that his main
goal in life is to locate his son—alive or dead. Patient +
wife will not rest until they have accomplished this.*

My grandfather's attendance at the hygiene sessions is erratic;
months slip by before he checks in with his doctors again. His
speaking tour for his son takes him away on weekends from his
remaining children and grandchildren, but he cannot stop himself.
As he goes from town to town, he waves the spoon he brought
back from Stalag 17 in front of increasingly smaller crowds as his
face grows flushed. "I was a prisoner of war and now my son is
one, too. My son was abandoned by the U.S. government."

9/12/85

Mental Hygiene Clinic

*Patient still has preoccupation with MIAs. Patient prefers
not to take medication for his nervous condition. He denies
any suicidal or homicidal ideation.*

When anyone suggests that he is unrealistic about his son's
chances of survival, he grows increasingly angry, reminding his
doctors and the people who question him that he is not a naive
parent but a former prisoner of war. The litany of things he's
seen is a rosary he recites to protect himself—and his son—from
sentimentality:

I've seen planes on fire and a man bail out and the
flaming gasoline ignite his parachute after it opened.
And I saw men thrown from a plane without a
parachute. I've seen a lot of guys who survived the
shoot-down and parachuted out, and a lot of 'em

were lynched or shot on the ground by civilians, and I've seen men be shot to death trying to escape out of Stalag 17. Some guys in Stalag 17 tried to commit suicide by cutting their wrists. So it's not a question of parents that are unreasonable and think that their son might be alive... but I think our government should be truthful. We want the truth from the government, that's all.

Any visions he has of his son's survival as a prisoner of war are violent ones drawn from life. But he prefers them to imagining his son's death.

15 / "Same-Same"

Who is more dangerous—an enemy that shoots back at you,
or a friend you cannot trust?
—Ed Pearce

Savannakhet Province, Laos • November 22, 2013 • Mom gone 4 years, 24 days

I'm shocked awake by the sounds of rustling bags and zippers
zipping. I sit up to find the night bus emptying around me,
my eyelids sticky from falling asleep with my contacts in. I feel
as though only an hour or two has gone by since we boarded the
bus, but the stiffness in my hips tells me otherwise: we have been
traveling for nearly nine hours.

Outside, the sky is deep navy punched with a million stars.

The Savannakhet bus terminal is little more than a covered
waiting area surrounded by a series of shuttered stalls and a
parking lot. Liz and I gather our bags and pick our way through
the trash-covered grounds, curling up on wooden benches to wait
for our guide. It's 5:30 A.M. and our guide is coming to get us at
6:00.

We last about five minutes before tiny bugs attack our skin
in buzzing clouds. We roll our suitcases across the lot, loud and
rattling in the emptiness, and pay 1,000 kip for toilets that I soon
discover are without toilet paper. When I emerge from the ripe
stall to wash my hands (without soap, of course), I realize there
is a basket with squares of pink tissue by the door and alert Liz,
who has been watching our bags, to not make the same mistake I
did. She goes into the stall prepared as I lean over the chipped sink

and attempt to brush my teeth with the bottled water we bought in Vientiane.

At 5:45 and again at 6:15 I call Mr. Bouk from our new Lao cell phone, my fingers clumsy on the hard plastic keys. Between the gnats and the utter emptiness of the station, I am growing anxious.

At 6:15, he picks up: "Almost there."

Click.

At 6:20 A.M., the sun now up, a white van pulls into the lot. We watch it go from puttering toy to actual vehicle, rust spots and all, as it slows to a stop five feet away from our shoes. Through the window, the man in the driver's seat comes into focus. His hair is slicked back in waves like Rhett Butler's—way too much effort before sunrise. His jaw flexes and releases as he stares at the road ahead, avoiding eye contact. The man beside him rolls down his window and waves.

"Hello!"

His voice doesn't sound like it did on the phone.

"Mr. Bouk?"

"I'm Mr. Ped, Bouk's brother." Traces of an uneven mustache stain the stranger's upper lip, competing with tiny beads of sweat. "And this is our driver, Mr. Tom." At the sound of his name, his slick-haired friend gives a movie star's nod before going back to examining his fingernails on the steering wheel.

Mr. Ped exits the van so quickly I barely register movement, and before I know it, he's reaching for my bags: "I know Sepon better than my brother does, so I will be taking you around. Get in, please."

Liz and I exchange looks. "Can you excuse us for a minute?" she asks. Liz yanks me aside: "I'm on board for a little adventure, but going into an unmarked van with two strangers in the middle of nowhere raises some *serious* red flags for me."

I agree. "This is how a lot of PSAs start." *And bad porn.*

I look back at the man alleging himself to be Mr. Bouk's brother. One finger is up his nose; the other is glued to a smartphone. He looks more Pillsbury Doughboy than criminal in his short-sleeved polyester dress shirt, but then again I haven't met that many criminals in my twenty-eight years. I glance at the horizon and see only beat-up houses and dusty roads.

"Do we have a choice?" I ask Liz.

Mr. Ped's phone rings—some theme song from a show I can't place—and he takes his finger out of his nose long enough to answer it. He rattles off a few words in Lao before handing it to me. The smartphone has the biggest screen I've ever seen, and I begin to wonder if it's actually a small video camera. *Smile, you're on* Candid Camera.

"It's Mr. Bouk," he says. "He wants to speak with you."

I gingerly accept his phone. The plastic is warm against my ear as the voice on the other end affirms what Mr. Ped has said, that Mr. Ped is his brother and that he hopes that is okay. I turn away from the listening group behind me to address the guide who's abandoned me with his sibling.

"I wish I had known sooner," I hiss-whisper.

"I am sorry. Something came up in Vientiane."

I wonder what could have possibly changed between our conversation just yesterday morning and now, but I return the slick smartphone to Mr. Ped and take in Liz's stare. We have two choices: stay in this abandoned lot or get in the van and get started.

Liz raises her eyebrows, and I nod. We get in the van with our suitcases in the trunk. We aren't even out of the parking lot when Mr. Ped again pulls out his oversized smartphone and begins to text. Even from the back seat, I can see the flirty emojis he's letting fly from his thumbs. *Is that a red kissy-lip face?* I look at the back of his head, his hair slightly gelled, as he chuckles to himself.

We have only forty-eight hours in Sepon, the longest I could afford to pay for the driver and interpreter on my journalist's salary. I want to learn as much as I can while I'm here, and I need him on my side.

I fire an opening volley: "How long have you been coming to Sepon?"

"For a long time." Text.

"Do you live here?"

Sigh. "I am from Vientiane, but I take tourists on tours."

"American tourists?"

"No, not many Americans. Thai and Vietnamese."

"And you work with your brother?"

He puts down the phone. "I want to open my own tourist company, but it's very expensive. You have to pay bribes."

"Bribes?"

"Twenty thousand U.S. dollars just to start. I just bought a house in Thailand near Chiang Mai and might base my business there."

"We just came from Chiang Mai! It's beautiful there; you're a very lucky man. Congratulations."

The faintest trace of a smile lifts his mustache before his phone buzzes and he bows his head again. The paved roads of Savannakhet proper are far behind us now. Red dust is everywhere, and the few motorcyclists and cart drivers who pass us wear masks to stop the dust from sticking in their throats. We slow at a snarl of trucks and see a paved highway of cement rising from the dirt alongside our own road.

Mr. Ped speaks up again, all on his own: "They say it will take two years to build a Lao-Viet highway. I say five. It's 120 kilometers long."

I tell him about the Big Dig in Boston and how it stretched over sixteen years and went $10 billion over budget.

"Not as bad as Lao-Viet highway," he concludes. Based on the condition of my spine after an hour on these roads, I'm inclined to agree.

He texts in silence for a while, then says something to the driver. He turns to us.

"Americans like coffee, yes?"

"Yes," I say. "Americans *love* coffee—especially these Americans."

"Good. I'll take you to the best place."

We drive for a bit before slowing by a sign in Lao that I ask him to translate:

"Seno."

Something is nagging in the back of my skull, a memory that is not my own. Coffee first, then I'll have time to think.

The van slows, and Liz and I step down to face an open building with a shaded roof and long, communal wood tables. A hefty man in a tight orange T-shirt is seated at a table. When he rises to shake hands with Mr. Ped, I see the English words across his chest: JUST DID IT, accompanied by a bootleg Nike swoosh.

"Hi, hi," he says, looking Liz and me up and down.

"*Saibaidee,*" I say.

Mr. Ped breaks into laughter. "They don't speak Lao here. They speak Vietnamese."

Just Did It joins him in his laughter. Mr. Tom remains silent.

"Sit, coffee is coming," Mr. Ped instructs, pointing at the table and saying something we can't make out to his friend.

Liz and I sit down. A little girl of four or five peeks out at me from the open doorway of the building as the man disappears into it.

"I think my grandfather was here," I tell Liz. "There was a refugee camp in Seno."

My mental picture of Grandpa drinking homemade beer with locals disappears as Just Did It returns with three glass cups, each with a stripe of sweetened condensed milk at the bottom and a tin structure on top, marked SAIGON, that coffee drips from.

The sound of a sputtering motor grows louder and its source appears: a man and two children on a motorcycle. He pulls off the main road behind our table. As the rider shuts off his engine and starts to dismount, I notice he, too, wears a colorful T-shirt: a yellow sickle and star on a red background. He helps the little boy and girl off the bike and smiles as he approaches our table. Mr. Ped greets the man warmly.

"Good friend," he tells us by way of introduction.

The man joins us at the table while his children wait shyly by their father's bike, taking turns peeking at us from behind the handlebars. A line from my grandfather's notes surfaces in my mind: *In Seno (just east of Savannakhet), one village chief thought he recognized the picture of an MIA as a man he had buried.*

Just Did It gets up to get more coffee. Mr. Ped and the man in the sickle shirt talk easily for a while until Just Did It returns with a plastic bag of dark liquid, which I realize is his to-go coffee. But as they talk, I hear a persistent hiss: the bag of hot coffee has sprung a leak and is dripping all over the table. I move to get napkins, trying to help, and they laugh and wave me off as Just Did It summons the small girl (his daughter?) to take away the leaking bag and get a fresh one.

Mr. Ped turns to us, all brusque in front of his friend: "If you need to use toilet, use it now. There won't be one until Sepon."

My stomach is all gurgly from the sweet coffee on an empty stomach. It's probably a good idea.

Mr. Ped says something to the young girl, and she points me toward an open doorway leading beneath the restaurant. I nod gratefully and descend the stairs. There is no back wall; it's an open basement, the dirty light streaking through from the open back of the hut, where a cooking fire smokes under a ripped blue tarp. As my eyes adjust, I make out tin pans and bowls hanging crookedly from nylon ropes. Toys are strewn in a corner—a truck, a headless doll. A calendar with pretty women, their skin covered to their necks, is pinned to a beam near a small temple laced with flowers. I realize with a small shock that Just Did It and his family must live here, beneath their business.

The only wall is a makeshift one to my right, and I reach for the doorknob slowly, afraid of what I'll find. I mentally rejoice when I spot the Western-style toilet but quickly sober up when I see the bucket of brown water with a floating bowl inside next to it. There is no other way to flush. There is no soap.

As I cross the front yard again, I see our driver sitting in silence at the table while the other men talk nearby. I walk over and try to engage him.

"Do you want any coffee?"

He stares at me blankly. I hear the sound of flip-flops approaching behind me.

"He doesn't speak English," Mr. Ped says. "Do you, Mr. Tom?"

Our driver looks down at his lap. Mr. Ped laughs at him, sharing in some secret joke with his friends.

"Can you ask Mr. Tom if he needs anything?" I ask, annoyed.

Mr. Ped speaks to him rapidly and the driver shakes his head and stands. He begins to walk toward the car, a slight limp slowing him down at each step.

"He's fine. Let's get going."

Back on the road, Mr. Ped asks if we liked the coffee: "Vietnamese coffee is very good, yes?"

"Very," I agree.

"I drank a lot of it when I was a student in Saigon."

"Saigon?"

"My father was a soldier. He sent me there to study politics."

"Oh," I say. This is new information. "It sounds like the best place to learn it, he must be very proud of you."

He laughs.

"Were you ever a soldier?" I ask.

"No, not me. My father wanted me to be in the police, but they don't want me for police. You ask people what they want to be in Laos, and they say, 'Policeman or army.' People are afraid of the police, but they respect them. I have a Thai girlfriend, so they don't trust me. You become police, people look at your life."

"I think I understand," I say. "My grandfather was soldier, then police."

My grandfather would have agreed with Ped: service is nothing without trust. Ed had said as much in an embittered op-ed to his "police brothers" shortly after his retirement:

> Having spent most of World War II in a Nazi POW camp, Stalag 17-B, from 1943 to 1945, I know much about war, dying and surviving. My experience as a PA state trooper for over thirty years gave me a realistic perspective on death, justice and the courts. All FOP [Fraternal Order of Police] brothers can relate to this. Since I retired in July 1976 my total effort has

been expended to learn the truth about our American MIAs. During the last eight years, my efforts have been hampered by the U.S. government.

Who is more dangerous—an enemy that shoots back at you, or a friend you cannot trust?

I decide then and there to trust Mr. Ped. "My uncle was a soldier," I tell him. "He came here."

"Oh?"

"I am very interested in the history of Sepon," I tell him.

The van grows very, very quiet; I can hear the taps of texts being sent from the front seat. I decide to leave it at that for now. More and more eighteen-wheelers with covered cargo slow our passage, kicking up dust in their wake. At several points, our driver actually dips into the surrounding grass to let them pass. Other times, he leaves the road just to avoid one of the hundreds of potholes that plague our way.

The sides of the road are devoid of trees, exposed to the sun. Mr. Ped points to a particularly big clearing in the trees and tells us, "They cut down and sell trees to China. Not good."

We stop by a marketplace still being set up. Faded tarps are stretched like skin across a series of metal arches, the crossbars dripping with netted bags of everything from just-killed crawfish to fattened cucumbers. A woman sitting cross-legged smiles at us as she arranges hand-carved bowls on a blanket.

"For monks," Mr. Ped explains, pointing at the bowls. I wonder if he is religious after studying in Saigon, a city where shrines and churches rest unattended, reminders of a spiritual past before Ho Chi Minh's rise.

We walk through the entire market in all of five minutes and are ushered back into the van. In no time, I spot the glimmer of what looks like a tollbooth up ahead.

"Police checkpoint," Mr. Ped says. "Have your passports ready."

"Checkpoint?" I look at Liz and think of the photocopied declassified documents in my bag—the maps, the reports... Will they see the Air Force seal and stop us?

Under the Lao criminal code, reporting news that "weakens the state" carries a jail sentence of up to one year, as does the act of merely importing a publication that is deemed by the government to be "contrary to national culture." Defamation is a criminal offense that can lead to jail time or even death.

A man in an olive-green uniform pokes his head through the passenger window and speaks with Mr. Ped. I focus on the blue tassels swaying from his shoulder, the braids pressed neatly around his arm. He steps away, then with a flourish slides open the van door. It whooshes on its track as warm air blasts our legs. The officer leans in, his eyes traveling from Liz to me, up and down. He's so close I can see myself in the black of his pupils. He exchanges a few more words with Mr. Ped without breaking eye contact with me, then laughs.

I jump when he slams our door shut before waving us on. When I look back, he is still watching us. He disappears in our trail of red dust, though the smile on his face does not. It takes a moment before I realize I'm still clutching my passport.

"You have to be careful with the police," Mr. Ped says from the passenger seat. He turns around to look at Liz and me directly. "My last customer, a Thai tourist, took a picture of officers at a checkpoint like this one. They locked him in Lao prison for a month."

I think I detect a faint tremble in Mr. Ped's voice as he speaks but realize I'm the one shaking.

In 2003, two European journalists were jailed while reporting on the war in Laos. The year after Liz and I travel there, Prime Minister Thongsing Thammavong will issue a decree banning "disseminating or circulating untrue information for negative purposes against the Lao People's Revolutionary Party and the Lao government." Internet service providers will be held liable for "tarnishing the Party," and citizens will be required to register for social media sites using their full names, making the sharing of news not sanctioned by the government almost impossible.

We continue to kick up dust as the rice fields blur by along the road, though now, the roadside is periodically dotted with shacks and people on motorbikes and wooden carts that hug the shoulder. When we come to five buildings in a row on a single street, our driver takes a right.

"Here we are."

We park before a sherbet-orange hotel complex that's only half built, a palm tree the sole plant in the dust of the yard. Construction workers hammer a roof on a set of rooms with wet paint.

"Biggest hotel in New Sepon," Mr. Ped says proudly.

New Sepon is called New Sepon because Old Sepon no longer exists, destroyed by the bombs my uncle helped drop. But while there are thousands of pounds of American bombs still in Lao soil, there is also copper and gold. In the twelve months prior to our arrival, ninety thousand tons of copper were extracted from Australian manufacturer MMG's Sepon mine alone. The precious metal is exported for rebirth as tubes and wires in Europe and Asia. The Lao government, a shareholder in MMG, sees mining as its main hope for overcoming the inflation and poverty that have plagued the country for decades. This Western-style hotel is a manifestation of that hope.

But mining in Sepon is nothing new. If you believe that geography is destiny, then the destiny of Sepon was written long before the original village was ever built. Human beings have lived in Sepon for over two thousand years. Nestled on the banks of the Sepon River and surrounded by subtropical forest, it's the former site of some of the most important burial grounds in all of Southeast Asia—and ancient copper mines dating back to the Iron Age.

Our driver kills the engine. I slide open the van door, Liz a few paces behind me. A woman who comes up to my waist runs out of the nearest building to greet us. I go to say hello and my nostrils fill with dust and wet paint smell. I promptly sneeze, narrowly missing her.

"I'm so sorry!"

She nods dismissively at my apology, then takes out a ring of keys and, without a word, begins walking swiftly toward the finished row of rooms. She turns to see if we are following her and I look from her to Mr. Ped.

"Yes, go. I'll wait here."

The key slides right in, and the woman opens a door to a sparse but clean room. A giant air conditioner with the tag still on it is installed in the ceiling. As Liz checks out the beds, I peek in the bathroom. It has a Western toilet, no buckets in sight.

"How much?"

"150,000 kip."

I do the math in my head: $25. The guidebook had placed rooms at $7.

"Are there any other rooms?"

"This is biggest hotel. Good for foreigner."

Liz and I confer with each other. The hammering has stopped as the construction workers stare. Everyone is looking at us. I walk over to Mr. Ped, who is waiting for us by the van.

"I'm terribly sorry, but, um, this is too much. Can you please take us somewhere else?"

Looking genuinely perplexed and still mumbling "biggest hotel in New Sepon," Mr. Ped says a few words to the woman who showed us the room before we pile back in the van.

We drive in silence to a second option. It's no less sherbet colored but smaller, the rooms danker, the bathroom with a flush toilet but also a bucket and a drain in the floor. The shower is affixed to the wall practically above the toilet.

"How much?"

"Sixteen U.S. dollars."

Well, looks like we've taken our last shower for a while.

Liz and I take two rooms, one for us and one for our driver and guide. At first Mr. Ped protests, but he eventually caves in. Surprise crosses his face as we hand him the keys to his little suite, just down the hall from ours. It's hard to know what will please him or catch him off guard.

We ask Mr. Ped to open the trunk of the van for us so we can get our luggage. His expression switches to confusion. He watches us roll our suitcases into our rooms without saying a word. I can't shake the feeling that something is wrong, and as Liz and I change and splash water on our faces, Liz says she feels something is off, too.

When we walk back outside, our suitcases tucked away in our rooms, Mr. Ped and Mr. Tom are in the van with the A/C running.

"Do you have your passport and valuables?" Mr. Ped asks.

"No, they are locked in the room."

He laughs. "I suggest you go back and get them."

I'm suddenly second-guessing not going with the "biggest hotel in New Sepon."

Sweat is forming on my upper lip as Liz and I return to the van with our worldly belongings in tow. The day is already hot, and it's not even nine A.M. We peel off the decaying "Main Street" and return to Route 9, the supply road that connected to the Ho Chi Minh Trail my uncle was bombing the night he was shot down. It's strange to think that Jack grew up on rural Route 6 in Pennsylvania only to disappear on another rural route, the 6 inverted to a 9, half a world away. I try to imagine Jack's plane above, the trucks moving slowly in the darkness where our van now shares the road with tractor-drawn carts and bicycles. The green of the surrounding rice paddies saturates my vision.

Our van bumps along until it slows in front of a placard saying OLD SEPON VILLAGE in Lao and English. A single red dirt road stretches before us, dotted with houses on stilts every few hundred feet. A bristled black boar grazes in the middle of the path, stomach swinging. She pauses to look up at our oncoming van before she resumes sniffing the dirt, as if she couldn't care less about our approach. We drive around her, the van's massive wheels sinking into the grass. It's only in the rearview mirror that I see the litter of pink-and-black piglets drinking from a corroded pipe behind her.

"The village of Old Sepon was completely destroyed by American bombs," Mr. Ped says. "Everything you see has been rebuilt."

I roll down the window, and the smell of warm piss and sweet hay surges into the van. The houses along the single road seem mostly vacant except for the livestock grazing in front yards of patchy grass. A young camel-brown calf rests in the shade of a rusted satellite dish. Nearby, a collection of worn T-shirts and men's boxers flap from a rope that runs from the sloping eaves of a hut to a sapling stretching up toward the sun. Most of the trees here look freshly planted, strikingly small compared to the mountains edging our view. We drive to nearly the end of the road and park.

The van doors slam as the four of us get out. A family that has been watching us from behind one of the stilt houses begins to walk quickly away, the youngest among them a boy of three or four who does not wear pants, his legs like matchsticks as he turns and grabs his mother's hand.

There is one figure who has not moved. From a distance, all I can see are the woman's deep blue garments swaddled around her as she sits beneath a house raised on stilts. I approach the clapboard house of silvering wooden slats. A few boards cling to blue paint, a long-ago nod to vanity. A green rusted truck of uncertain make is parked beneath the house. As I pass it, I notice a Benji-like dog without a collar roaming beneath a laundry line that sags in the heat of late morning.

I'm only a foot away from her now. The old woman before me is sitting mermaid-style on a raised platform painted the same color as the house above. Her dusty bare feet are tucked under a traditional Lao skirt, the cotton dyed navy with fine stripes of red and cream. A gold chain reaches from her neck to breasts hanging loose under a red tank top with two buttons done up—the most skin I've seen exposed on a Lao woman. Her arms are brown and rippled, and she looks at least eighty years old, though a lifetime in the sun or a lifetime of heartbreak could place her at sixty. My heart races regardless. *She is the right age to know something.*

I hear Liz and Mr. Ped approach behind me. I turn to him and ask, "Can we talk to her?"

He says something to the stranger in Lao and she responds, still staring straight ahead.

"She is blind," Mr. Ped says.

White wisps of hair float like clouds across her expressionless face as she raises it to me. She nods, waiting for the next question. The woman was born and raised in Sepon, the house above her rebuilt on the same plot as her childhood home. She lived in the caves across the river from 1970 to 1975, during the American bombings. I asked how they lived, how the children learned, how they ate; she said the Viet Cong gave the people food.

When I ask my guide to see if she remembers any American prisoners during the war, the capturing of any planes, he pauses before turning to her. Her voice changes, a beat lower, as words tumble out. She shrugs, then her shoulders still.

Mr. Ped translates: "There were so many bombs, so many planes. We lived in the caves. We knew nothing. All same-same. Nothing more."

I thank her and ask to take her picture, and she assents. As I raise the camera, she straightens, continuing to look at a point on the horizon we cannot see. Mr. Ped says a few words to her and motions for us to go back to the van. I continue to glance at the blind woman and the family staring at us a few hundred yards away from the shadows of a second house, closer to the river. I want to talk to them, too, but Mr. Ped seems nervous, eyes darting around. He says something to our driver and turns to me: "We go to see Northern temple?"

I look at Liz, and she shrugs. As we climb in the van, I turn to my friend and voice my concern that we are being hustled through town.

She echoes my inner dialogue: "We can come back. We have two full days."

Out here, we are at the mercy of our driver and guide. Forty-eight hours was all the time I could buy, and I can already feel the seconds drifting away from me. I'd spent four years researching this place, imagining what it would feel like to stand on this exact spot on earth, and I feel like I'm being rushed away before my feet have even touched the ground.

We drive slowly back down the bumpy main road and park before a row of cement monuments rising out of the grass. One has a broken-off top painted indigo blue and crusted with red clay; another has traces of yellow and blue next to an earthen stupa shaped like a mini Pha That Luang. Outside the car, Mr. Ped gestures to two big dips in the grass between us and a row of graves. The pits are one hundred feet across and perfectly round.

"From American bombs."

As he points, we hear laughter and look beyond the craters to see a group of schoolchildren running in our direction. They wear white collared shirts with navy skirts and shorts that just brush their knees. A few carry bright parasols to block the sun. As we watch, they continue to emerge from a low white building— the schoolhouse, Mr. Ped tells us—and gesture at us across the craters.

If they knew who we were, they wouldn't smile and wave so warmly, I think. Not for the first time that day, I feel an incredible sense of guilt.

The craters are deep and jarring; the lip of one is mere feet from the front door of a hut, a laundry line with child-sized Superman pajamas strung across the chasm. Nearby, the beams of a new home rise just beyond the rim of another. My eyes travel down into the waving grass, where something white catches my eye. At the base of a wide, twisting tree—one of the oldest I've seen in the village—pyramids of sand rise like sand castles smoothed by waves. White twine has been wrapped around each mound and a single string connects their peaks. Between them, someone has placed a porcelain plate holding dozens of honey-colored candles that stand in a thin layer of water. Small puffs of white flowers float in the liquid, the water reflecting the branches above.

I ask Mr. Ped what it means, and he says it is an offering to the full moon. I wonder if similar piles of sand were knocked down the night Jack's plane fell, the mounds turning to craters.

Turning left, we circle Old Sepon's still-under-construction wat. Five Buddhas stand between the craters and the temple. The mustard-yellow paint on them is fresh and bright against the grass. Mr. Ped directs our attention behind us to a brick doorframe that stands alone, an entry to nowhere. He tells us that this was once the reinforced entryway to a vault used to store payment for French soldiers. I draw closer and see an infantry of ants crawling on the shelves, now bare of bills and open to the elements. Grass and a few flowers sprout from the top layer of crumbling brick. It is unnerving to think of French men here; this land feels so remote, like it has nothing to do with the rest of the world that exists beyond the mountains.

As we walk away from the temple, we pass another sign next to the one announcing Old Sepon. It's written entirely in Lao, but the images require no translation: sets of skulls and crossbones flanked by bombs with red exclamation points border the text, a warning about what still lurks beneath the soil.

Liz, Mr. Ped, and I make our way up "Main Street," this time on foot. On our left, construction workers swarm behind thick, grand gates. We pause to watch them work. The frames of three red houses rise from the clay, joined by walkways. The complex is large even by Western standards and thrown into relief by the surrounding one-room houses on stilts. The scrape of shovels and the hammering of nails echo across the street.

"Who is building such a big house?" I ask Mr. Ped.

"The president's wife is from Sepon. He is building this house for her," Mr. Ped says.

I take in the rising red beams, the fat fence around the property. My eyes travel across the street to a home that is worlds away from the new construction it faces. Two graying wooden huts on stilts are connected by an open platform and swooping garlands of drying laundry, limp in the sun. The whole home seems fragile somehow, as if the ropes of drying shorts and weatherworn T-shirts are holding it all together. I am reminded of a story that fascinated me as a child about a little girl with a green ribbon around her neck. All of her friends asked her why she never took it off, but she didn't answer them until, sick and in advanced age, she permitted her husband to remove it—causing her head to roll off her shoulders.

My sneakers crunch loudly on gravel as we make our way farther down the street. *There aren't even any birds here.* Aside from the occasional sound of a hammer, it could be a ghost town. I try to picture this place abandoned after the war, craters left to the breeze sweeping from the riverbank and up into the mountains that sheltered the villagers from the bombs that destroyed their homes.

We are at the town's convenience store now, little more than a hut with plastic bags of prepackaged food dangling from the eaves like cotton candy stalls at a carnival. A woman of fifty or so is seated on the stoop of the store with a child, still in diapers, in her lap. The child reaches his brown arms up to us and smiles, all gums.

Mr. Ped pauses, then rushes toward the woman and hugs her. They speak rapidly in Lao. When he remembers that we are behind him, he turns and tells us, "She was a friend of my grandmother. They grew up together. My grandmother is dead now."

He didn't tell us he had family here. I flash back to his face as we drove up, lips pressed together under his mustache, his silence as he stared into the crater.

Mr. Ped turns back to the woman and they speak in earnest, words tumbling over one another. I stand there, feeling as fragile as the house I'd seen, unsure of myself, of my right to be here, of my qualifications to ask these people about their lives. The baby is still smiling at me from the shade of the porch, and that is something. I kneel down, level with his big black-brown eyes. We exchange funny faces, a wordless dialogue, and for a moment, I lose track of the adults and the huts and the unexploded bomb warnings around me.

There is a rustling by my ear as Liz reaches into her bag and pulls out one of the plastic cars she picked up in Vientiane. She looks at Mr. Ped, who is now staring back at her.

"Is this okay?" Liz asks. She looks into the older woman's eyes and motions with the car.

The woman nods.

"Yes," Mr. Ped says.

Liz approaches slowly and puts the car down on the steps to the convenience store. The baby lurches forward and, prize secured, claps and laughs in appreciation. All we see from then on are the ends of his thick eyelashes, his attention consumed by the plastic car he runs back and forth across the wooden porch.

We are all silent as we watch him play. I am the first to speak. "May I ask her a few questions?"

I smile at the woman, but she does not return my gaze. I think of the voice recorder in my purse that I have brought for this purpose, then look at the woman and Mr. Ped. I need to earn their trust. A recorder might seem intimidating. I don't reach for it.

"Please tell her I want to learn about what happened here," I say.

Mr. Ped turns to her and translates. She nods without looking at me.

"She is okay, yes," Mr. Ped says.

I introduce myself and ask for her name, how long she has lived here.

"All my life."

"Were you here during the bombings?"

"Yes."

"Can you please describe what your life was like during that time?"

She looks from Mr. Ped to me, then raises her arms in the air. For the next five minutes, she speaks rapidly, swishing noises and explosions and planes in the sky painted with her fingers.

Mr. Ped's translation is two sentences long. "She knows nothing. All same-same."

I have the sense that he is leaving a few things out. I decide to press on.

"Do you know if Americans were ever captured here?"

Mr. Ped pauses, blinking at me.

"Please," I say.

He nods, then speaks to her. She gestures again for a while, pointing at the mountain, then folds her hands in her lap.

"Know nothing, all same-same," Mr. Ped says.

I'm not convinced. "Is that all she said?"

He looks from her to me. "She says the Vietnamese came ten years ago and took American plane parts for museum."

Plane. Singular. "Museum? What museum?"

"They are building a war museum in Da Nang."

I look at the woman, and she stares at the dirt in front of the porch.

"Time to go," Mr. Ped says.

"But I—"

"Now."

I glance from the woman to Mr. Ped. She is watching intently as the child plays quietly with his pink plastic car. *Is she afraid?* Liz gets up and stands next to me. The plastic wheels rattle back and forth against the floorboards.

"Come on."

As we walk away, Mr. Ped leans close—so close I can smell sweat mixed with his breakfast—and tells me, "Viet soldiers paid villagers a visit recently. Told them not to talk about the war."

I recall the frightened looks on the faces of the families watching me speak to the blind woman. I turn back in the middle of the street. The woman we just spoke to is staring at us. Our eyes lock, and she shakes her head at me before returning her gaze to the child.

16 / White Christmas

There's the constant doubt—is he still alive? You think about how many Christmases is he over there? How many Thanksgivings, when the family is all together? When you're alone at night, you're wondering, "Is he suffering? Is he sick? Is he still alive?"

—Ed Pearce

*M*om watches me from the couch as I sift through the pile of old VHS tapes on the living room floor, trying to find family videos that will lift her spirits. Behind me, the fire Dad made for us before he went to bed is dwindling down, throwing arms of light across Mom's face. The two-story windows Mom had designed for this room never quite shut out the chill of the woods around us, but I have to admit that on nights like tonight, they let in the full power of the moon hammering light onto the snow, making the tops of the pine trees that rim the yard seem like construction paper cutouts of themselves.

I find a tape that looks older than all the others, its label marked simply WEDDING. I hold it up for Mom to see and she takes it, turning it over in her hands.

"I thought we'd lost this," she says, her eyes fixed on the tape.

"Do you want to watch it, Mom?"

She looks up at me, eyes twinkling under her chemo cap. "I have to show you your old mom was young once, too."

I shove the tape into the VCR and climb onto the couch next to her. Her bare feet are cold against my leg and I tuck the afghan around them carefully. "We've Only Just Begun" by the

Carpenters starts to play on a black screen that suddenly bursts into light with the date: May 19, 1979. I lean forward and watch as my grandparents' beat-up brown-and-taupe 1968 VW camper rolls up to the curb outside St. Patrick's Church in Milford, the world around it green from a spring rain. The door slides open and a hand and white lace sleeve appear, followed by a face. Mom steps onto the wet pavement, nearly tumbling out in her long white dress. She looks like something out of a Victorian novel: lace buttoned up to her throat, billowing sleeves, and a train of white she holds aloft to keep it from dragging across the damp ground.

She slams the van door and steadies herself, then looks up—straight through the camera—and throws her head back in a laugh, rows of white teeth like sails, her jaw the prow of a ship coming into harbor. She draws her hand to her face, too late to hide cheeks glowing pink with embarrassment. When her head drops, a blur of baby's breath is visible, woven into the honey blond of her hair. We both watch as younger Mom disappears up the steps of the church and out of sight.

The camera shifts and my grandfather appears on-screen, looking young and tan. He takes his daughter's arm in the vestibule of the church, his broad shoulders dwarfing her own as he walks her through a sea of friends and family. At each stained-glass window, the light reveals an extra shine to Mom's eyes—both father and daughter are close to tears, but neither will let themselves cry. Ed hugs his only daughter and joins her hand with my father's.

I sneak a look at Mom on the couch beside me. The light from the TV screen plays across her steroid-round cheeks, but her eyes are dry, as if they'd dried up a long time ago.

After Mom's death, I learned that she had wanted to wait until Jack was home so he could be one of the groomsmen in gray tuxedos escorting her college roommates, Denise and Sheila Marie, down the dim aisle of St. Patrick's. Instead, he was declared dead two months before her wedding day. She was now older than her big brother was when he disappeared, and it must have been disconcerting to get married before and without him. It was only when I learned this that I began to understand something more of what the camera caught rolling across her face as she scanned the full-but-empty church before turning to the man she was about to marry.

Linda Pearce Rotondi on her wedding day. May 19, 1979.

Milford, Pennsylvania • December 24, 1984
Jack missing 12 years, 8 months, and 25 days

Jack's dog tags arrive on my grandparents' doorstep on December 18, 1984, a week before Ed and Rosie's twelfth Christmas without their son. The candles flickering from every window in the dusk are overpowered by a giant sign in the front yard visible to anyone driving down Route 6, one of the two main roads in town. It reads: PRAY AND WORK FOR THE SAFE RETURN OF THE MISSING IN ACTION

IN SOUTHEAST ASIA. The sign is framed by five small American flags and a pennant with a logo reading, POW*MIA: YOU ARE NOT FORGOTTEN. MIA bumper stickers cover the VW camper parked in the driveway, the miles it's driven on behalf of the missing as hard on the van as they've been on my grandparents.

From the La-Z-Boy in the living room, my grandfather can see the candlelight reflected in the glass ornaments Rosie has hung on the family Christmas tree. My grandmother inherited the ornaments from her mother, and only two of the original glass balls remain after the childhoods of Ed and her five kids.

My grandmother has stayed up for the past few nights wrapping gifts, tucking them between the bottom branches and the candy-red tree skirt she'd sewn when the children were small. The tree is already starting to dry out; periodically, pine needles fall on top of the paper with a soft *plink* as the radiator hisses.

The package that arrived via certified mail was not wrapped, yet the sense of anticipation Ed felt when he signed for it left him as breathless as any child.

There is a difference, Ed was discovering, between hearing that your son's dog tags have been located and holding them in your hand. The reality of them against his skin—objects that once touched his son—moves him in a way he doesn't know how to admit. His wife is the Catholic one, but the tags feel like some type of relic to him, as if a part of Jack still flowed through them. I feel the same way when I hold them now, the cold metal with Jack's last name—my middle name—pressed into my palm.

The sequence of events that brought them across the world is dizzying, stretching longer than the beads of the missing chain that once connected them to Jack's neck. The first report containing information about Jack's dog tags was filed in 1983, four years after my grandparents had begged to keep their son's case open at the hearing in Texas. A slip of paper with Jack's name was passed from a refugee at Na Pho camp to the camp nurse, the string of letters—EDWIN J. PEARCE, 192387175, A POS, METHODIST—illegible to her, copied down from a metal tag she claims she didn't possess.

The letters snaked their way via telegram to Bangkok, Vientiane, and then the White House. Jack's name, blood type, and religion lingered on paper for a year in the capital, landing on the desks of the secretaries of defense and state before finally being reported to Ed and Rosie. When questioned, the government didn't elaborate on how the refugee came to pass along Jack's identifiers like notes in class. But if that first source didn't have the physical tags at the time, who did? The document is heavily censored, silent on the things Grandpa Ed—and I—wants to know most.

The second report arrived a month after the first was declassified. It promised not just information but "remains": "[Redacted] ref provided information on the remains of two alleged remains, Bodine, Robert Jr. and Pearce, Edwin J. These remains were allegedly being held by Lao Resistance near Na Pho camp."

When Ed visited the refugee camp in '73, the families had been huddled together, their bombed-out homes smoking in the mountains. Were the tags snatched from Jack's body, copied down, and circulated in an attempt to barter information for food? For extradition? Ed knew better than anyone what a man would do to ensure his family's survival.

In March 1984, a consultant and translator for the National League of POW/MIA Families called with news. Ed went straight to the papers:

> Milford, PA—The dog tags and remains of a Milford, Pa., serviceman missing since his plane was shot down over twelve years ago might have been recovered from the crash site, a Vietnamese woman told the man's family.
>
> Last week, Le Thi Anh told Edwin and Rosemary Pearce, parents of Air Force Staff Sgt. Edwin "Jack" Pearce, that she had seen the purported evidence in late February. Ms. Anh said she was shown the tags and a pound of bones, including teeth, during a

February 24–25 visit in a Thailand jungle hideaway by guerillas fighting the Communist Laotian government.

Rosemary bagged lunch meat at the Grand Union by the pound and produce by the half pound; a pound of bones and teeth belonging to her son seemed too extraordinary a thing to bear. When I first read these details in my mother's papers, I dreamed of bags of teeth for months.

Ultimately, the tags Ed holds in his hands this Christmas Eve were returned not by his government, not by refugees, but by Jack Bailey, a private American citizen. My grandfather knew Bailey's name and reputation before the tags even arrived. The whole country did.

People magazine called Jack Bailey the "American Don Quixote of Thailand" for his crusading on behalf of refugees displaced by the war and the way he defied governments in his pursuit of leads on missing Americans. Bailey's latest turnover electrified the country. But he wasn't so popular in government channels; Bailey told reporters he had Jack's dog tags, "three small packets of alleged U.S. remains," and two other pieces of bone *before* he notified the JCRC, the government group Ed had met with back in '73 in charge of excavating all crash sites and graves for American remains.

Bailey originally turned Jack's tags over along with a bag of "human and non-human (pig) bone fragments," the paucity of which, the government report concluded, "preclude the development of any ID or anthropological data."

The bones were a dead-end. But the dog tags in Ed's hands were the ones his son had worn around his neck when he took off that night and entered the sky.

On November 17, 1984, as Rosie planned her annual Thanksgiving menu—green bean casserole and a turkey large enough to feed twenty—another report surfaced, contradicting the earlier two: "Source, a 27 YOA male, provided hearsay information

concerning alleged U.S. POWS detained in Laos during 1984...
Source stated that he had <u>heard about seven other POWS held in
the Sepon area</u> (see attached name list)."

In the attached list, "SSGT Edwin J. Pearce" is listed twice.

Ed read his son's name and felt both victory—*ALIVE!
ALIVE!*—and a gnawing unease. Under what conditions? Did he
know what plants to eat to keep his belly full, to not make eye
contact with the guards, to do all the tiny things that can lead to
survival—all the things his father and the Air Force had taught
him? Between March and November, my grandfather had seen his
son transform from a bag of bones to a living man in captivity. He
refuses to break faith.

The government feels otherwise. The report claiming Jack is
a POW in Sepon is accompanied by a letter from the Air Force
rebuking its authenticity. It's fabricated, officials claim, based
on the repetition of Jack's name, likely compiled "using dog
tags which they [refugees] have scavenged from crash sites or
purchased from other refugees in the camp." Knowledge about
missing Americans, when shared with the U.S. government, could
feed entire families in Laos.

There is a stirring on the stairs; Linda and her husband—my
parents—are visiting from Massachusetts this Christmas, sleeping
in Jack's old bedroom upstairs, the two twin beds pressed against
the wall. My grandparents have converted my mother's first-floor
childhood bedroom into a mix of war room and museum housing
the boxes and boxes of documents they are accumulating about
Jack.

I imagine my grandfather watching his daughter descend the
stairs. In photos from the period, Mom's permed dark blond hair
is wild to her shoulders, the roots just growing out. She is thirty-
one years old and recovering from her third miscarriage. I won't
be born for another year.

When I think of them in that room, backlit by the Christmas
tree covered in tinsel, I find myself focusing on my mother's hands,
the ones I held as a child and, later, after chemo. I imagine my

grandfather depositing the cold metal tags into her open palms. Her fingers running over the letters embossed in aluminum: EDWIN J. PEARCE, A POS, METHODIST. They sit in the dark room and pass around Jack's dog tags instead of a grandchild.

17 / Just Pray

The Pearces admit their search has robbed them of the ease of retirement years and the chance to devote a fair amount of attention to their other children. But they also say they can't stop looking for their son.
—*Pocono Record*

Savannakhet Province, Laos • November 22, 2013 • Mom gone 4 years, 24 days

*M*r. Ped walks quickly ahead of us, guiding us away from the homes of Old Sepon to what he calls the "Northern temple." I'm not done asking questions, but I need to stay in Mr. Ped's good graces, so I follow along a few paces behind him.

"*Saibaidee!*"

Mr. Ped has stopped before a house on stilts so high, it could qualify as a tree house. A homemade ladder reaches up from the patchy grass to a dark open doorway. I squint up to see the person Mr. Ped is calling to. A pair of dusty brown feet dangles over the ladder, then the corner of a saffron robe. I hear laughter as the face of a teenager comes into focus, light acne dotting his cheeks. He and Ped exchange a few words, then he shouts to someone inside and begins to climb down the ladder.

At ground level, the young monk is about five feet five inches tall. He smiles shyly up at Liz and me and motions with his hand that we are to follow him. Liz, Mr. Ped, and I trail him to the building behind us. It's a single-level structure built on a cement foundation, a roof of corrugated metal streaked with red rust. The exterior wall facing us is covered with a blackboard the size and style of the one in the COPE Visitor Centre. Instead of

"Impossible Is Nothing," this board is covered in seventy-eight numbered phrases in Lao. The only thing I can read are the numbers that precede each line.

On the red tile steps behind the board, a bald boy of five or six in a monk's robe sits, taking us in. His playmate, in gray rubber sandals and a soccer jersey, runs up and down the steps around him.

"I have something I want to show you," Mr. Ped says, looking at me.

The noonday sun is high above us now as I follow Mr. Ped around the building. We pass a gleaming silver water tank that throws the sun back in our faces—the shiniest thing in town by far—labeled VIET. I squint in the glare and the back wall of the building comes into focus. Tiny round holes radiating cracks cover its entire surface. In some areas, larger circles of missing plaster expose an underlayer of ruddy brick.

"Many bullets passed through this wall. It was one of two structures still standing after Sepon was flattened by bombs. They rebuilt the temple around this single wall."

I approach it and run my fingers across the cool plaster, feel the jagged edges of the holes. Mr. Ped watches me do so, then gestures for me to follow him.

We're at the steps now; the child monk is gone. In silence, we remove our shoes and enter the temple. It takes a moment for my eyes to adjust to the windowless room, lit only by the doorway and the gap between where the bullet-ridden wall meets the peaked roof, a radiating triangle of light that perfectly frames the giant gold seated Buddha before us.

"The Buddha was unharmed by the bombs. The people here believe he has magical powers," Mr. Ped says.

He looks up at the Buddha and I follow suit. We kneel side by side on the carpet, hands clasped, alone with our thoughts. I can hear Mr. Ped's shallow breathing grow slower. He closes his eyes.

As we stand to leave, I see a framed photo of a young man on the floor among a jumble of candles and offerings. I know I've seen his face before.

"Who is that, Mr. Ped?"

"Souphanouvong."

Souphanouvong, the half brother of Prince Souvanna Phouma and Prince Boun Oum. I had read about him and his family when I was researching mine. Born to a prince of Luang Prabang and a commoner, his education in Vietnam led him to become a disciple of Ho Chi Minh and, later, to lead the Lao People's Revolutionary Party as the "Red Prince" in opposition to his brothers. Another family torn apart in the name of war.

Back in the sun, I notice how close the temple is to the river. My mind is still buzzing with news of a museum just across the mountains in Vietnam—a museum that might have my uncle's plane in it—and the face of a communist leader at the feet of Buddha in a temple pocked with bullet holes.

The splash of a water buffalo easing its body into the river to drink not fifteen feet from where I'm standing brings me back to the present. I look from the giant animal back to Liz and our guide waiting for me up by the half-built temple rising out of the jungle. Mr. Ped's eyes dart from the construction workers in short sleeves eating lunch farther down the bank to the parked van two hundred meters to his left. He seems eager to leave.

What would Mom do?

I ignore Mr. Ped and walk toward the picnic table of men, the tiles they're adding to the temple piece by piece in piles around them. A few begin to point at me. Cans of Lao beer are scattered around the table along with the remnants of noodles. The tallest man at the table nods at me. I try to talk to him, the Lao coming out stilted: *"Saibaideebor?"*

Have I said it right?

I try again. The men seated at the table laugh at the butchered Lao phrase coming out of my mouth. I think of Mr. Bounmith's note in my pocket. *Would this be the time?* Mr. Ped is out of earshot, and I hear the van's engine start up; this may be my only chance.

"Miss Jessica. Miss Jessica. We leave now?"

I turn and Mr. Ped is walking toward me, the van door hanging open behind him. He wants me in the van. Immediately. I nod and smile at the men, who break into laughter again, pointing at my legs. I feel their eyes on my back as I walk away.

"How did it go?" Liz asks once I'm safely in the van.

"We have to come back," I say, watching the temple, then the town, growing as small as I feel in the rear window.

"Go back?" Mr. Ped turns around to face us from the front seat. "We are not going back to Old Sepon."

"Wait. Why? We paid for another day." My voice comes out an octave higher than normal. We are almost at the end of the last dirt road now, rice fields swallowing up the view of the schoolhouse.

"Police will ask too many questions if they see Americans asking questions like you asked today," Mr. Ped says. "People will talk."

I should have asked him to stop. Gotten out of the van. Begged him to turn around. Explained myself. *This is my only chance to talk to these people. If I come back again, everyone who remembers the war will be dead.*

But what can I say? I can't drive here, I can't speak the language, and I am at the mercy of this guide-brother I wasn't even supposed to work with.

Liz and I traveled across the sea and land and mountains and were granted a little over an hour in the one place I'd been circling on maps ever since I saw the word "Sepon" in the newspaper clippings in my mother's papers. Liz rubs my sunburned shoulder, but when I glance over I can tell that she is as shocked as I am.

As the rice fields sway in the heat outside the polarized van window, I think of my grandfather all those years ago, bouncing along in a military jeep in search of Jack. How it must have felt for him to turn around, just seventy miles short of his goal, and go home empty-handed. If I can't get answers in the village, there is one place left on this earth my grandfather would have chosen to go, and that's where I will go, too: Jack's crash site. The coordinates are burned into my memory from my mother's papers.

I direct Mr. Ped to tell the driver to head toward the mountain.

Campfires are beginning to bloom along the roadside as we leave Sepon. The setting sun shooting through the mist that clings to the mountains ahead is beautiful, but it also means we're running out of time. My body is buzzing with the need to get to the mountain before dark. I need to see if the roads leading up it are accessible, how far into the jungle we'll need to hike tomorrow to get to the crash site.

We turn left at a large sign in front of a village. Mr. Ped points out a large statue to our left surrounded by a fence. The village is vibrating with motorcycles and people carrying bags of rice and bottles of water to and from small, squat buildings that line either side of the road. From their porches, bright packages glimmer from inside clear plastic bags that have been hoisted up and tied to posts. Above several of them, plastic tarps stamped with cell phone ads—the local brand Unitel is ubiquitous—stretch across thatched roofs that, if not for the modern advertising, would not seem out of place in the last century.

A white wall signaling a temple rises to our left, and I try to stare through the courtyard's trees to see the temple itself, but the darkness and the thick branches block it like a curtain. I slide the back window from right to left and Mr. Ped yells, "No cameras!" A policeman is driving by on our right. I jerk my arm back in as his car passes. The ruts in the road through the village are deep, and our spines vibrate in tune with my desire to go, go, go, though we cannot drive above twenty miles an hour. Children dart in and out of our path on foot and the occasional bicycle.

Once the village is behind us, the road ahead is clear, and we get a good, solid glimpse of the mountain before us. It's old and eroded, lush with green leaves sucking at the mist.

"How much farther?" Mr. Ped asks.

I sneak a look at our coordinates on the satellite phone. Lie. "Not long now."

Ten minutes later: "It's almost too dark to see, how much longer?" he asks.

"Not far."

There are no lights but our headlights on the trees, which seem to close in as darkness falls. We cross a wooden bridge stretched over a ravine, the clatter of wood from loose beams so loud I fear that at any minute, we'll be pitched into the water below.

"Let's hope there aren't any more bridges along the way," Liz whispers, her nails digging into the van's cloth seats.

By the time we cross our third, then our fourth, then our fifth bridge in this condition—wooden beams sliding and shifting beneath the van's weight—Liz and I resort to squeezing each other's hands. Liz keeps her eyes shut, but I can't stop staring. Every stream we cross, to me, could be the stream that runs through the crash site on my grandfather's maps, the water running beneath these bridges from the same source that once flooded the wreckage, scattering plane parts and bits of bone forever.

A sudden break in the encircling trunks shows the setting sun reflecting off a canopy of green. We are high up now, higher than I had imagined. It almost seems as if we had flown to this elevation, the valleys below shimmering beneath the van windows.

I think of the bird's-eye view report of the crash recorded by Captain Howard Rowland, who observed the missile's impact on Jack's plane from the air:

> The explosion appeared to be an airburst which seemed to tumble and fall to the ground and continue to burn... We did not observe any missile launches, but Capt. Lumsden and I did observe a thin, vertical smoke trail up through the moonlight.
>
> At approximately 0305 we received a SAM activity light and a light launch. We dove to avoid further acquisition and departed the area... Shortly after the explosion we heard a distress beeper on guard frequency. As we were leaving our working area we obtained approximate UHF DF positions on the

beeper. The beeper appeared to be coming from the
general area of the crash site.

"We need to turn around," Mr. Ped says, pulling my focus
back into the van.

"There should be a road on our left coming up in a few
moments," I tell him.

In the darkness, all four of us lean forward. Then, to our left,
the trees open up. The road is there.

Liz and I open the window and stare out. It's dirt, like the
roads behind us, but it looks passable by car.

"Far enough," Mr. Ped says. "We are turning back."

Liz and I look at each other and exhale. *The road exists. We can
make it.*

"Yes," I relent. "We can turn around for now."

Our driver throws the van into reverse, and we back into the
trees, nearly dangling over the edge of the mountain, headlights
throwing light into the darkest jungle I've ever seen.

The road back seems faster than the way up, but it could be
that my anxiety has finally given way to some semblance of hope.

Mr. Ped turns in his seat to look at Liz and me. "Are you
hungry for dinner? Do you eat noodles?"

I'm so thrilled that we found the road that it takes me a
moment to register that Mr. Ped is talking about our next meal.
"Sure."

"You are going to love my friend Lu's," Mr. Ped says, clearly
in a better mood.

Is his attempt at conversation an olive branch? An apology for
his prior behavior? I try to observe his face, lit up by his phone's
screen and reflected in the windshield. He is smiling at a message
I cannot see.

Back on Route 9, the moon is full over the pitch-dark roads,
the only view out the window the occasional burn of a far-off fire
to indicate that we are not alone. Our van circles back along the
bleak strip of road that is New Sepon, the restaurants—the only

huts with signs, three of them blinking KARAOKE—all dark inside. We park outside a small hut with wooden tables out front. As we are seated, I notice there is a hole at the center of our table and a charcoal pit beneath.

"You know barbecue?"

"Yes," I say, confused.

Mr. Ped is grinning wider than he did when we naively left our passports in our hotel room.

A teenage girl comes over. She smiles at us shyly before lighting the charcoal beneath our table. I watch, curious, as she places a big tin bowl with an upside-down strainer in the middle over the flames. She pours a kettle of steaming broth into the bowl and brings plates of red raw meat—"Beef from Thailand," Mr. Ped translates—and oblong white plates of cilantro and raw eggs with bundles of dry glass noodles.

"Watch driver," Mr. Ped says.

Mr. Tom, still a mystery to us after spending hours together in a snug van, offers a rare smile—*This stuff must really be good,* I think—as he opens the package of dry noodles and upends them into the just-boiling water. I watch his face illuminated from the fire below and try to read it. He can't be much older than us. I wonder how he came to work for Mr. Ped and why he speaks so little, even with his coworker. He looks up and, for a moment, his deep brown eyes catch mine. Just as quickly, his expression closes off again and my view is reduced to his still perfectly styled hair.

"Where do we go tomorrow?" Mr. Ped asks.

"Sepon?" I try again.

"No Sepon. Cannot go back. No more questions."

I frown. Fine. Two can play at this.

"Then back to the mountain," I respond.

"What's in the mountain?" he asks.

Our driver skewers a piece of red beef with a chopstick and holds it above the hot coals, causing it to hiss.

"Remember when I told you my uncle was a soldier?" I ask.

"Yes." Mr. Ped cracks a raw egg over the bowl, and the rich yellow yolk slides into the broth.

"He was flying planes over Laos. His plane was shot down over the mountain. I want to find the crash site."

Mr. Ped stares at me unblinkingly, realizing I'm much more than the average tourist I pretended to be. "The mountain is in a national park forbidden to foreigners," he says. "Police will not allow it." He pauses, staring at me. "I cannot let you."

I open my mouth to counter, but Mr. Ped interrupts me.

"You paid for Old Sepon. You pay us for extra gas up and down the Ho Chi Minh Trail and back and forth to mountain?"

I look at Liz, and she nods at me over the fire. "Yes," I say. "Yes."

But despite it having been his own suggestion, Mr. Ped shakes his head. "I don't know. It's not a good idea."

I can sense his hesitation. I need to show him he can trust us and that the mountain is worth fighting for. I turn over our day together in my mind and land on the one time we had been on the same side: on our knees in the bullet-ridden temple.

I think of my grandfather's World War II–era prayer book in a drawer beside my bed at my apartment in Brooklyn. I take it out when I miss Mom, unsure of what to do with the fragile pages. My grandfather believed the prayers saved him when he was in Stalag 17. Mom believed they could protect her from her cancer.

"Mr. Ped," I begin, "my uncle was missing for thirty-six years, and for all those years, we had no body to bury. This site was the last known place he was seen alive."

Mr. Ped raises his eyes to me, considering my face.

"I just want to go there and pray," I tell him. "So I can bring peace to my family. Will you let me pray there, for my family?"

He blinks at me, the smoke rising from the fire between us. "Just to pray?" he asks.

"Just pray."

Mr. Ped holds up a finger and slides the plastic chair away from our table. "I'll call my brother."

His cell phone flashes blue, like a struck match, before he holds it to his cheek, the glow of his cigarette fading to an ashy stump in his fist as he puffs and paces, paces and puffs. All I can focus on is the rhythm of his flip-flops hitting the dirt. *One, two, three, four, five* paces right, *one, two, three, four, five* paces left.

He gets off his phone and comes back to the table. I pretend to be suddenly very interested in cooking a piece of meat, though it keeps slipping through my chopsticks and into the murky broth.

"You pay extra," Mr. Ped says.

I nod.

"We go."

I look up at him, eyebrows raised. He nods.

"American girls are crazy. Police ask, you are from Canada, okay?"

Liz and I laugh and nod empathetically. "Understood." I have the urge to jump up and hug him, but I am afraid to do anything that will make him take those magical words back. "Thank you. Thank you so much."

For the rest of the meal, he barely touches his food. I, on the other hand, can't stop eating.

Back at the hotel, I look over at Liz, her shoulder rising and falling in the twin bed beside mine. Above us, the fan whirs, shooting shadows across the wall. I should be exhausted, but all I can think about is what we'll find on that mountain.

18 / *Archaeologists and Undertakers*

Mr. Pearce was very concerned about the lack of effort in finding
men missing in action. He said General Kingston [and the] JCRC [are]
just a bunch of archaeologists and undertakers.
—Air Force Casualty Branch call log, September 13, 1973

Milford, Pennsylvania · March 7, 1986
Jack missing 13 years, 11 months, and 7 days

*T*he photo in the March 1986 issue of *National Geographic* is
unbelievable. It shows a propeller taller than a man rising
from the ground, surrounded by metal twisted like the car wrecks
Grandpa Ed used to be called to clean up as a Pennsylvania state
trooper on Route 6's climb up the Poconos.

But the photo was taken on another mountain in a country a
world away. And the propeller is from Ed's missing son's plane.
I picture my grandfather pulling the black plastic frames of his
glasses higher up his nose, as if he can somehow change what he's
seeing in the milk glass light from above the dinner table. He holds
the magazine inches from his face, crumbs from the table cutting
into his elbows.

February 18, 1986. Systematically, step-by-step, a
United States Army team examines what's left of the
four-engined U.S. Air Force AC-130 whose call sign
was Spectre 13—seeking what can be found of its
fourteen-man crew... after nine days the yield includes
some 5,000 bone fragments, many no larger than a

rice kernel... The U.S. team considered its mission a success. True, the human remains recovered are scant. The plane's high-speed impact and secondary explosions took their toll. And this site, like others in Laos, had been disturbed, not only by local villagers taking what was obviously useful, but also possibly by American adventurers and assorted Southeast Asian mercenaries on illegal cross-border forays from Thailand. Despite discouragement from all governments involved, bones from such crash sites have been sold in Bangkok. One American reportedly paid $30,000 for what he was told were the remains of his son.

According to the U.S. government, it's been fourteen years since anyone has seen Jack's plane, and there it is, in full color, for the consumption of subscribers of a magazine known for topless photos of natives and wild animals. Ed could have howled.

In one *National Geographic* photo is the dirt-crusted dog tag of the plane's infrared sensor operator, Richard Castillo—my grandmother's friend Betty's husband. In another, one of the men involved in the excavation holds up a pocketknife and a revolver covered in red clay as if they were relics of ancient Greek pottery.

In the final full-color photo, rusted propellers rise, half buried in the jungle, as a team of Lao workers, their backs to the camera, walk away.

At the Army's Central Identification Laboratory in Honolulu, forensic experts made lengthy analyses. Some sixty teeth and fragments proved almost as valuable as fingerprints, for they can be checked against military dental records. Of Spectre 13's fourteen crewmembers, six identifications have been made—subject to confirmation...

Ed doesn't get the phone call until September—six months after the *National Geographic* article is released—that one of those sixty teeth is, according to the government, Jack's. And officials are leaving the decision as to whether to accept the tooth as Jack's mortal remains up to our family.

My grandfather is far from ready to accept it. "The government was going to send that tooth [to me] in a seven-foot coffin, flag-covered," he tells the *Philadelphia Inquirer*. "A front tooth doesn't mean a man is dead." How many times had he taken his son to the dentist and brought him home whole?

The Central Identification Laboratory (CIL), the group in charge of identifying remains on behalf of the U.S. military, claims the tooth is Jack's for several reasons: because it comes from a "known limited population flight crew" and is a closer match to his dental records than the records of the other men who were on the plane that night, and because "the presence of CMSGT Pearce's identification tags in the vicinity of the remains."

Yet the assumption that everyone on the crew perished on impact is contested by the eyewitness report saying nine men were rescued. Dr. Samuel Strong Dunlap, a forensic anthropologist working on the case, alleges that his boss at the lab tried to coerce him into making scientifically insupportable identifications:

> We had a few "meetings" at which Furue and Helgesen [the men in charge of the lab] tried to get us to come up with a statement or agreement that all the men the army said were on the plane <u>were</u> on the plane even though we did not have the hard evidence for it (skeletal or dental) or even circumstantial evidence such as dog tags or firearm serial numbers. If this isn't fraud I do not know what fraud is.

Dunlap says that the recovered material was mishandled and that small items—especially teeth—were not properly labeled when removed from the earth. Without knowing where bones and teeth were located in relation to each other and to the plane, he argues, critical information about what happened during and after the crash is lost for good. Dunlap is so disgusted with how the remains from the crash are being handled that he leaves the CIL to file a formal complaint with the secretary of the Army.

On September 10, 1986, the heads of the CIL are brought before the Investigations Subcommittee of the Committee of Armed Services in the House of Representatives. They face allegations that they falsified records to make positive IDs. Three independent forensic anthropologists present the results of their investigations. The first anthropologist finds 50 percent of the CIL's cases to be misidentified, the second 66 percent, and the third, Dr. Charney—the man who had called to tell Ed that one of the discovered teeth was Jack's—90 percent misidentified.

"That is more than just the terrible problem of having the wrong person in the family grave. That is a question of writing off people who might be alive," Dr. Maples, the second anthropologist, tells Congress.

Two MIA family members make explosive claims from the Senate floor: Jerry Dennis, brother of Mark V. Dennis, and Kathryn Fanning, wife of Hugh Michael Fanning. Jerry buried his brother Mark's casket unopened when it came back from the Air Force a month after his shoot-down in July 1966. Then *Newsweek* ran a photo of Mark as an "unknown POW" in November 1970. Jerry exhumed the body he had buried in his brother's grave; the skeleton was five foot five. His brother was five foot eleven. Kathryn was told her husband was identified by his skull and teeth, then exhumed his body to find that the casket did not even contain a skull.

My grandmother writes to her friends about Fanning's case:

> She is a Marine wife and up until 1982 (I think) she thought the govt. was A-OK. Then she asked to see her husband's file after they had sent her a bunch of bones... including a skull and teeth (by which he was

identified, or so they said). In her husband's file she found several papers listing him POW! She was astounded. When she went back to the Air Force room to see them again, they were removed. They told her she didn't see what she saw. She had her husband's grave exhumed and there was no skull! Lies Lies Lies! It seems a close parallel to our story.

Ed isn't a scientist—far from it—but even he can see the facts don't add up. He holds on to every word from the witnesses, seeing in their testimonies what he's been saying about government officials for years: *Frauds. Liars. All of them.*

In 1987, the CIL shocks Ed when it retracts its statement that Jack's dog tags were found at the crash site. The tags, it turns out, were *not* found in the vicinity of the plane but returned by a private citizen... something Ed has known all along.

When the dentist who identified the single tooth as Jack's hears that the dog tags were not found near the crash, he makes the radical step of rescinding the positive identification... but it is too late for the Air Force to change the rubber stamp it had put on Jack's papers after the 1979 status review hearing declaring that he'd been killed in action: "Mrs. Pearce, we surely understand your feelings and your reluctance to accept a single tooth as tangible evidence of your son's death. However, the identification of your son's remains has no bearing on the finding of his death, which was established by the Air Force in 1979 with the passage of time."

1/15/87

Mental Hygiene Clinic

Patient concerned about blood pressure. He used to be on meds, but it caused muscle cramps. He spoke about MIAs in Laos and how gov't is telling lies. He's admitting he's close to his breaking point.

In 1998, Ed will sit with Rosie at the dining room table that was once his command center in the search for Jack, using a regular kitchen spoon to lift his daily breakfast of cornflakes to his mouth. The room around him will begin to grow warm as the blood clot in his neck pushes against his artery, plugging the flow of blood to his brain.

My grandmother tries to catch her husband as his chair falls back and his head collides with the floor. Rosemary dials 911 while Ed's body jerks. She doesn't yet know her husband will never walk or speak normally again, felled by the blood echoing too fast in his head.

A year after his stroke, I will interview my grandfather about what he did in the war for a school project. When I press "record" with a polished neon-green nail, I can hear the tiny wheels on the tape recorder start to tick as his sentences stretch out like the parachute he is struggling to describe: *I jumped... into... the... sky. The Germans... were coming... at us fast... I was falling, falling....*

19 / Let Go

They say that you are born alone (although, as a mother, I would argue that point) and that you leave this world alone. I just want to say that after that initial moment of hearing my diagnosis, I have never felt alone again.

—Linda Pearce Rotondi

Milford Cemetery • Milford, Pennsylvania • September 20, 2008
Jack missing 36 years, 5 months, and 22 days

I am twenty-two years old and wearing black for a man Mom won't talk to me about, though she squeezes my hand and Morgan's as we walk with her from the car to the cemetery. Mom's steps have been shaky for months. Her right femur was replaced with a titanium rod when the cancer spread to her bones, but she is surprisingly fast as she whips across the uneven grass toward a woman with a camera around her neck. Mom lets go of our hands to hug the stranger and introduces her as a local newspaper photographer here to take pictures of the service. I pause to see if I have heard her correctly: *Pictures of a funeral?* But Mom is already leaving us behind to greet Grandma Rosie. Morgan and I lock eyes behind Mom as if to say, *What is going on here?* We excuse ourselves and hurry to catch up with her.

"Linda." My uncle Kim wraps his big arms—broad at the shoulders, just like Grandpa's—around Mom and pulls her into a bear hug even tighter than their normal greeting. Uncle Kim's head is mostly bare now, the long reddish locks he once wore as a sign of protest gone along with years of anger, though in that moment, all I know is that he looks tired. From behind, the two could be mistaken for twins as they hug. They share the same height and haircut now; Mom's blond hair is just starting to grow back after chemo as his recedes.

Uncle Kim pulls away and whispers something to Mom that I can't hear. She nods. I hover a few feet away with Morgan as Uncle Kim takes out a walnut box so small it fits in his left hand. I'll later learn the twelve-by-twelve-inch box had been escorted from a lab in Honolulu to Stroyan Funeral Home in Pennsylvania by a chief master sergeant from the Air Force—a man the same rank as Jack.

Mom and Grandma Rosie draw closer to Uncle Kim as he takes a screwdriver to the bottom of the box.

In the letter that accompanied it, the Air Force said it contained "a metacarpal (incorrectly designated as a proximal phalanx in the AFDIL report) [that] can be attributed to CMSGT Edwin Pearce on the basis of mtDNA testing." My mother had had to look up "metacarpal," her fingers typing in the word only to learn it meant just that, "finger."

Her brother's hand.

Jack's crash site was excavated for the second time in 2006, during my senior year of college. While I was away at school, Mom was contacted about submitting a DNA sample for testing against the remains. The undetected tumor was already spreading to her lymph nodes as her DNA was compared with the DNA from the bone shards pulled from the jungle and transported to a lab in Honolulu.

The second phone call came in 2008. Mom had just completed her clinical trial at Dana-Farber Cancer Institute and was awaiting news of her latest bone scan when the Air Force called to say a rare mtDNA mutation in her blood matched the mtDNA from the bone fragment. Officials believed it to be Jack's.

As it did with the tooth in 1988, the Air Force left the decision to accept the single bone shard as Jack's mortal remains up to his surviving family members. And after thirty-six years, we were given only two months to either accept or reject it.

Mom and her remaining brothers held secret late-night phone calls to try to decipher the reports together. Grandpa Ed had died on New Year's Eve 2005 at the age of eighty-three, believing his son still lived. With Grandpa Ed gone and my grandmother already in the early stages of dementia, it felt strange to give up on Jack now. Or was this their final and only chance at peace?

Mom had recently retired from the Red Cross, giving her a lot of time to think—perhaps too much time. Though she did not discuss her disease or her missing brother with her children, her Valentine's Day card to my father that year revealed just how much the decision and its timing weighed on her:

> Chuck,
> When I get upset over the problems that we come across, you calm me. When I am too sick to care about myself, you comfort me. And when I am depressed about my brother, you soothe me... I love to cuddle up next to you in bed when I feel so cold and you feel so warm. I guess what I'm trying to say is I love you and always will.
> Love,
> Linda

In the cemetery in Milford, my uncle pries open the box's lid as my grandmother leans forward in her wheelchair. If this is what is left of her firstborn, Rosie wants to see it.

Inside the box are layers and layers of cellophane. Kim unwinds the tiny sheets to find a yellowed one-inch piece of bone. A small hole has been drilled midway through, stuffed with bone dust encased in more cellophane—the sample that was taken in 2006 and compared with samples of my mother's blood and found to be a match.

The packet that had accompanied the remains was as thick as the one sent in '72 when Jack went missing, full of dense diagrams and incomprehensible paragraphs. Mom had contacted my college friend Steph, who was getting her master's degree in forensic anthropology at NYU and sifting through World Trade Center remains, to ask if she could help translate it.

In September, Steph drove up from New York City to sit with my mom and eighty-three-year-old grandmother at the small round table in the kitchen. The last of Mom's hydrangeas bloomed between them as she went over the report with them until they understood.

In Milford, the look on my grandmother's face as she peers into that box is one of lucid pain. With her husband gone, she leans into my mother for support. Uncle Kim closes the box, and Morgan and I step aside to let the three of them pass before following our family out into the sunny September afternoon. We don't yet know we'll be burying Mom within the year.

> Dear Stephanie,
> Without your explanation of the DNA sequencing, which gave me the confidence to accept the government's findings regarding Jack's remains, we might still be searching for answers. After thirty-six years, it is still hard to accept that Jack will not be walking through the door, but it will be easier for us all to heal now, knowing that he is finally home. Jack was lost in 1972, when I was a college freshman. Now I am middle-aged and not in the best of health and you have given me back my big brother.

The wind picks up and roars through the leaves along the side of the mountain, their vibration sounding like ocean waves to my ears. We make our way single-file through the graves to Grandpa Ed's. A fresh hole has been dug beside his plot for Jack, much smaller than one for a normal grave.

My mother and my grandmother hold hands in front of me as members of the Air Force color guard march around our family. They wear the uniform my uncle once wore, brass buttons shining in the sun, polished black boots crushing the grass.

My grandmother receiving Jack's flag and medals.

Mom has already written the inscription for the gravestone her brother and father will share:

SEPARATED BY A GENERATION,
FOUGHT IN DIFFERENT WARS, BOTH SHOT DOWN FROM THE SKIES.
THE FATHER, A PRISONER OF WAR, RETURNED TO FALL IN LOVE,
RAISE FIVE CHILDREN AND LIVE A LONG LIFE.
THE SON'S REMAINS WERE RETURNED THIRTY-SIX YEARS AFTER
HE WAS SHOT DOWN, TO BE LAID TO REST WITH HIS FATHER,
WHO HAD NEVER STOPPED SEARCHING FOR HIM.

Above us, a far-off droning sound turns into a rib-shaking thrum. I jump as the thick underbelly of a giant plane passes overhead, casting a shadow over all of us. I feel a hand on my shoulder. "It's an AC-130," Uncle Kim whispers. "The plane Jack was in the night he was lost. They're flying it just for us."

I look down at my mother, her eyes still on the sky, her stubbled crown catching the light. Three volleys of shots pierce the sky over Pennsylvania, commemorating the dead. As the airmen gather the spent shell casings from the ground, two dragonflies hover in the air above our family. They linger above us briefly before darting off into the trees, their wings reminding me of the airplane that just thundered over our heads.

The shell casings are wrapped in an American flag and presented to my grandmother by one of the airmen, his white gloves spotless in the sun. The flag he hands her is bigger than the box we just buried.

For Valentine's Day the following year, Mom's last with us, she gives my sister and me a photo album. Inside are blurry pictures of a plane in the sky and the Air Force color guard saluting a tiny hole in the ground. At the time, I didn't understand why anyone would make a photo album of a funeral—much less give it as a gift. That album was the closest Mom ever came to sharing what bringing Jack home meant to her with her daughters. Perhaps after almost forty years of writing letters and waiting, she had simply run out of words.

20 / The Crater

I feel certain that he's alive and that he will come home,
and I'll never give up that thought. Never.
—Rosemary Pearce

Savannakhet Province, Laos • November 23, 2013 • Mom gone 4 years, 25 days

*T*he sun rises over the rice fields, and from the van window, Liz and I can see the red roads and green rice paddies blurring toward the mist fleeing the mountains. Liz tries to manage my expectations; even if the smaller roads are passable, the likelihood of finding the crash site beyond them is slim.

We have no idea if we will be sent back from the park's border by police—or worse. Mr. Ped has instructed us to say, "Tourist, tourist," and smile if we are stopped. Even if we do manage to make it through, we have no idea if there are unexploded bombs or impenetrable jungle blocking our way. The highways here require herculean navigation, never mind the spidery network of roads crawling up the mountain.

I brace myself for the first of the bridges. A calm pervades the van as we clatter our way over it. Easy. The scary part is up ahead. The van slows, and I peer out the window. We've come to the police checkpoint guarding the perimeter of the park. We slipped by easily enough last night, but daytime is a different story, Mr. Ped had warned us. I suck in my breath and scrunch down in the seat. The checkpoint is eerily quiet, the wraparound porch bare. A sleeping mutt lies just inside the open doorway; he doesn't even raise his head as we pass.

I wait until I can no longer see the building in the rearview mirror to exhale. The road up the mountain becomes a green tunnel. Every few hundred feet, the trees open up to reveal blue sky and a sheer drop to the valley below. The effect is dizzying. We take a left just after the clearing from the previous night, and the van rattles down an even thinner red clay ribbon of road.

The van lurches, then stops. "No further," Mr. Ped says.

"What? Why?" I ask.

"The road is too bad. Cannot pass."

Our driver begins to turn around. As the van slows in reverse, I slide the door open and jump out.

"Wait!" I yell.

"Get back in the van," Mr. Ped says.

Before me is a waterfall of mud, dropping down steeply to the rutted, grooved remains of a road. I have no idea how I'm going to get down it, but I'm sure as hell not getting back in that vehicle and driving away.

"I'm walking, Mr. Ped," I announce. "You can stay here if you'd like."

I slam the van door a little too loudly, and it reverberates out into the jungle around me, trees barely held back by the red clay trail. I adjust the weight of my backpack. I have enough water to last a few hours; if the terrain remains relatively steady, I can make it.

"You can't walk into the jungle alone," my guide says. "You don't know this place."

Watch me, I think. I start heading for the point where the road dips from view.

"The police will find you!"

A second van door slams as Liz comes to stand beside me.

"I'm walking, too."

"No, no. American girls cannot be alone in the national park."

I hear Mr. Ped's heavy breathing, a muttered phrase in Lao that sounds a lot like "fuck," a third door sliding open. He comes around the van and stands before Liz and me, blocking the way. "If you go, I go with you," he says.

I look up and down his five-foot-one frame. In his flip-flops, dress pants, and semi-tucked dress shirt, Mr. Ped won't last an hour.

"How far?" he asks, pointing at the jungle ahead.

I think of the nearly forty-year-old map in my pocket. Of the grieving girl of the past four years who could barely navigate her own life, let alone a map. Of the nine miles that stretch from where I'm standing now up into the mountain. I lie and say three kilometers.

"You have twenty minutes," Mr. Ped says. "Then we leave."

Liz and I look at each other. "Well, we'll just have to walk fast then, won't we?" she whispers.

We move almost sideways down the hill to keep from falling face-first. Loose clumps of red dirt tumble down with each step, and I try to still my heart's pounding by focusing on the dried ripples of mud beneath my feet. Behind us, the sound of Mr. Ped's swearing grows fainter.

On flat ground and already well ahead of Mr. Ped, Liz and I form a plan.

"I'll talk to him; you just walk as fast as you can," she says.

She hands me the satellite phone, the black digits on the screen showing me just how far away I am from home—and just how close I am to the coordinates of the last known place my uncle was seen alive. I think of Mom marching up to the Lao embassy in 1975 in search of her brother, the road I now stand on marked off on the map in her purse.

Liz's footsteps slow behind me as I pick up my pace, each footstep matching the thudding of my heart. *Jack, Jack, Jack.*

Above us, the sun is rising higher, extending its fingers down to the road. The world is so red, I feel as if I could be walking on the surface of Mars. I bake along with the dirt.

I hear footsteps and slow as Liz catches up to me; Mr. Ped has agreed to give us a full hour. I don't know what she said, but the smile on her face as I show her the satellite phone reading—a few more decimals in the right direction—says it all.

"Jess, if the road continues up, we can potentially do this."

We double our pace.

Power lines swoop high above our heads, and I recall our guide's fear at seeing them so deep in the jungle. The roads encircling the mountain, he had told us, are trafficked by loggers illegally removing hardwood trees from the forest to sell on the black market. We look as out of place as the power lines above us.

Liz and I round a corner, and a solitary man appears in the middle of the road, walking straight toward us. His chest is bare, his face covered in dirt. He's three feet away, then two. I can see the mud in his curling toenails.

"*Saibaidee,*" I say, smiling.

Liz elbows me. His face parts into two rows of brown teeth as he returns our greeting, stepping aside at the last minute to let us pass.

"Did you see what he was carrying?" Liz whispers.

I turn and see a giant machete strapped across his back, glinting in the sun. Spooked, I reground myself. I look up at the mountain, taking a swig of water that sticks to the back of my throat. We walk on in renewed silence, my every sense heightened. The gravel behind us begins to crunch under the weight of tires. The pop and crackle slows and comes to a stop just behind my legs. I can feel the heat from a car's engine shooting hot air down the back of my calves.

Shit, the police, I think. *It's over.*

I turn around slowly. The tinted window next to my skull momentarily shows cheeks draining of red sunburn and filling with white. My cracked lips disappear last as the window rolls down to reveal the laughing face of our driver.

"Get in!" Mr. Ped calls from the passenger seat. "Crazy girls..." he mutters under his breath.

He has no fucking idea.

As we slide the van doors shut, Mr. Ped explains, "It's better to have car and all be together if asked to leave. You do *not* want to ride in police van."

He looks uncomfortable at his own joke, and I continue to look at him. After a beat, he admits, "It's also too hot to walk, okay?"

I could hug him. The adrenaline is still pumping through my body, and the four of us driving together, even if only for the A/C on his part, feels like a leap of faith in our mission. In me.

As we drive, the coordinates on my satellite phone screen get closer and closer. By pointing the antenna out the open van window, we can obtain a reading roughly every five minutes. A few hundredths of latitude off, we see a series of huts too small for human habitation rising out of a murky pond to our left.

"Are those to hold prisoners?" Liz whispers.

"For storing rice," Mr. Ped shoots back from the front seat.

We are startled that he has heard us, that he was listening in, that he has understood. I recall the back seat conversations Liz and I had while he was playing with his phone, his translation of "know nothing" in Sepon, and begin to question just how much he has masked what he does and does not understand.

A few hundred yards beyond the rice huts, a village comes into view. I blink to see if it's a mirage. We are within a mile of the site now. I had pictured uninhabited remote environs, not huts rising out of rice fields...*rice fields*! The Air Force said the crash site had been periodically flooded for rice farming. The people before us could be the farmers.

We slow where the two roads in the village converge in front of a sign I cannot understand. It is wooden with white painted letters fading in the sun.

A woman ducks away from the roadside where she'd been watching us, retreating to her doorway, a toddler clinging to her leg. Mr. Ped rolls down his window, tries to say something to her. She shakes her head.

"They don't speak Lao," Mr. Ped says, "I can't understand them."

By now, a group has gathered to gawk at the van in its midst. I recall the declassified report from my mother's papers:

A former North Vietnamese Army lieutenant serving in Savannakhet Province, Laos, reports seeing two captured Americans as they were tied behind a truck and dragged through the village. He surmised that the Americans could not have survived the torture. [Redacted] stated that it was common knowledge in the capturing unit that the two Americans were captured the night before when their C-130 was shot down....If this report is true, it is possible that [redacted] saw two survivors of the March 1972 AC-130 loss.

"Roll up your windows, now," Mr. Ped instructs. We do, watching the villagers' faces grow darker behind the tinted glass. We need to move. Our driver throws the van into gear and we go about fifty feet before we come to a second crossroads. Straight ahead, the path rises and disappears into the trees. To our left is a small wooden bridge crossing a stream. The satellite phone has gone dark, the signal blocked. We have to choose.

"Take the bridge, please."

We lurch forward, and as the huts grow smaller behind us, Liz prays aloud that the road keeps going in this direction. We need to move north to draw closer to the coordinates. As soon as we are out of sight of the village, she rolls her window down again and lifts the satellite phone outside of the van, extending the antenna as far as it will go toward the horizon.

When the next reading comes, it brings bad news: the road is snaking farther and farther away from the coordinates, the decimals dropping.

I see a small footpath and point it out. "Should we get out here and start walking?"

Half of me is afraid I'd dreamed it, but when we pull over and kill the engine, the path is still there, just wide enough for a body to slide through. I have no idea how far into the jungle it will take us or where it leads.

Liz, Mr. Ped, and I get out. Liz is about to close the van door when I dash back in, grab my camera, and train it on the woods. I barely feel the branches scratching at my bare arms as we wind our way through the trees. I'm reminded of the warnings in my guidebooks, echoed on the plaque I saw in Sepon: DO NOT GO OFF OF TRAILS; UNEXPLODED ORDNANCE IS STILL A THREAT.

I am walking toward the last known location of a plane laden with bombs—and guiding my friend right to it.

The deeper we go down the trail, the thinner the trees above us become. I can feel the sun beating down on my head as our shadows stretch long before us, announcing our arrival to the tiny white flowers at our feet.

Just as suddenly as the jungle had swallowed us up, the cathedral of trees parts. Before us is an abandoned rice field drying in the sun. I imagine a rusting propeller, a man's watch face, a severed hand entwined in roots.

We slosh in, our sneakers making a sucking sound as we leave tracks in the mud. Liz gallops ahead, satellite phone antenna quivering in the air, trying to get a signal.

Everything before us is the color of hay, of the Buddhas of Sepon. Two buzzing specks dart across my field of vision, followed by a pair of shadows casting a familiar shape in the grass: dragonflies. I think of the dragonflies stitched on the hospice quilt that covered Mom and the ones that circled my family as we stood over my grandfather's grave.

The dragonflies circle me once, twice, three times and then dart off to my left. I know it's crazy, but I begin to follow their flight path, stumbling as I try to make out their shape in the heat. I gesture for Liz and Mr. Ped to follow.

A buzzing begins to build over the field like a fire alarm. I have the unsettling sensation that we've traveled back in time, that the sound is coming from emergency beepers with antennae extended up toward the sky. That Jack is lying near the field. That if I get there in time, I can save him.

I think of the Air Force report wired to Washington, D.C., the day after the crash: "It is possible for some of the crewmembers of Spectre

13 to have bailed out... the possibility of their survival still exists."
As we approach the edge of the field, the buzzing of cicadas stops.
The land is very dry here, our feet stabbed by the rice plants
shooting up from the uneven ground. The *crunch, crunch* is jarring,
like stepping on bone.

The path has run out now. The dragonflies are gone. It's just
Liz, Mr. Ped, and me in a maze of young trees. I am reminded of
Alice and the chessboard in *Through the Looking-Glass*, wondering
what each square I choose has in store. I know, too, that somewhere
on this board are the remains of Jack's plane. A branch scrapes my
upper arm, and a thin line of blood darkens against my skin.

Mr. Ped steps ahead of us, stops, and points through the trees
to our right: a red crater sinks sharply about thirty yards away.

"Jess, I think we are on your map," Liz says. "This has to be
one of the craters."

I step into an indent in the ground. Clumps of bubbled
and blackened earth rise out of the red clay, looking like the
dried skin of some long-extinct dinosaur scooped out of the
surrounding jungle. Two hundred meters away I spot a sliver
of brown water splitting rocks. I know in my heart it's the creek
from the map, receding back into the forest in the heat of dry
season. I call Liz over and we follow it a ways, crossing at its
narrowest point.

The creek drops off into a crater stretching out before me in
every direction. It's a giant fire pit, but instead of charcoal clumps,
rocks as large as my body are blackened into a crust and scattered
in a pit six feet deep.

Nothing grows here. There is no wind. The sun beats down,
and I walk around this desert in the jungle, looking for traces
of Jack. Deep, circular holes are dug into the crater walls, as if
something has been recently pulled away. I recall what the woman
in Sepon said about the Vietnamese taking the "American plane"
away for a victory museum in Da Nang.

"Jess! Jess!" Liz yells across the crater. "I've got the coordinates.
We're here. We're on top of the crash site!"

I see a glimmer of white and bend down to the red earth: a perfectly smooth snail shell, a curling nautilus. I see another. And another. The entire base of the crater is scattered with bleached shells, the remnants of a moment when it was underwater.

A strange, low wail fills the air, and I realize I'm sobbing, my body shaking so badly I drop the camera clutched in my fist.

Liz and Mr. Ped rush toward me. "Okay? Okay?" he asks.

I can't speak.

"Picture?" Mr. Ped asks, uncomfortable. I can feel the snot dripping from my nose, the fat tears pouring down my face. Liz puts her arm around me and we stand, the crater around us. Mr. Ped squats to snap the picture and stops to pick up a blackened pebble. He holds it out to me.

"Bone," he says, placing it in my palm.

I hold the small, hard object and try to calculate how long it would take to run to the rice fields, for the villagers to see who had been shot down, for them to find a scared twenty-four-year-old in the forest.

I think of the search party circling above, antiaircraft fire spraying up like fireworks. Of the giant American plane that returned the next day to bomb the still-smoking AC-130, the bombs on the ground and the ones from the sky carving and recarving the hole I now stand in. Of the people in the village eating rice watered with rain that once fell on a plane full of bodies, then bones, the pieces breaking up and floating away.

Mr. Ped draws closer to me. "I didn't believe you, but you showed me faith. I see now. You have faith in your family."

I begin to laugh in the middle of the crater, tears still running down my face.

Liz takes my camera and points it at me. "I want you to always remember how you feel right now."

The last time I let myself cry, I was walking behind my mother's casket, the box buoyed on the shoulders of her surviving brothers, her nephews, and her husband, carried out into the New England sun.

"I wait for you," Mr. Ped says, backing away to give me privacy. Liz follows.

I run my hands along the edges of the crater where the earth has fallen away, study the roots starting to shoot down, perhaps one day to reclaim this barren patch of exposed dirt.

I want to call Mom and tell her we finally did it.

I want to hold my grandfather's hand and guide him to this very spot, fill our pockets with shells.

I want to ask Jack where he's been all this time. Let him know how long we've been looking. How hard we all tried.

I stand still and feel the blood of my grandfather, my uncle, and my mother rush in mine.

The Pearce family. From left to right: James Michael Pearce ("Mike"), Robert Timothy Pearce ("Bob"), Rosemary Pearce, Kim Pearce, Edwin Jack Pearce ("Jack"), Linda Pearce (later Rotondi) and Ed Pearce.

Epilogue

I went to Laos hoping to learn something my grandfather had not. I left still not knowing how Jack died or when, or if any of the suspicions or hopes my family had held for almost forty years were true.

But when Liz and I drove back down the mountain that day, I was not wondering if Jack went down with the plane or if he was one of the men allegedly pulled alive from the wreckage in 1972. I didn't ask myself if the dog tag reports in my mother's papers meant he was held prisoner somewhere beyond my grandfather's reach, as my family had always believed.

What I felt instead was peace.

My father told me that when my mother was pregnant with me, she woke up one morning and had a strange feeling that Jack was dead. As if one day she could feel her brother's presence and the next could not sense him in this world. That was in 1985.

"Was she sad?" I asked Dad. "Was she scared?"

"She felt calmer," he said. "Like she could stop holding her breath and get ready to watch you take your first."

I will never fully know why Mom didn't talk to me about Jack. At his funeral, I knew only that he was her big brother and that he never came home. There are conversations we will never have and things we will never share. My wedding day, like hers, will be half empty. She will never meet her grandchildren. When I lost Mom at twenty-three, I desperately wanted a message from her, a set of instructions about what she wanted me to do in a world without her. What I got instead was the chance to meet her at my age.

In *The Year of Magical Thinking*, Joan Didion's memoir about losing her husband and daughter, she writes, "I know why we try to keep the dead alive: we try to keep them alive in order to keep them with us. I also know that if we are to live ourselves there comes a point at which we must relinquish the dead."

The mountains in Laos don't look so different from ours. Their rivers, either. What I realized in my time among them is that no matter how far you travel in this world, your inner world comes with you. For the Pearce family, that means the people you love never really leave; they just walk around inside your chest, and it's up to you how heavy their footfalls press on your heart.

My uncle Jack was trying to become his father when he rose up in that plane on March 29, 1972. I had spent the past four years trying to become my mother. What neither of us perhaps realized was that we can't relive things for the people we love; all we can do is try to understand them, love them, and know when to let them go.

The author and Liz at Jack's crash site.

Acknowledgments

Thank you to Elizabeth Dickson McNamee for accompanying me around the world and being the smartest and bravest companion on overnight bus trips and treks through the jungle of my family's complicated history.

To Jordan Turgeon, my first editor and champion, who lived and breathed this book almost as much as I did: thank you. This book wouldn't exist without you.

I'm forever grateful to Allison Hunter at Janklow & Nesbit for never giving up on this story or the people in it.

A huge thank you to my editor, Olivia Taylor Smith, for helping the truth about what happened in Laos live forever.

Thank you, Dad, for raising me to ask questions of the world around me and for reminding me of the people who made me who I am.

Thank you to my sister buddy, Morgan Elizabeth Rotondi, for reading countless versions of this book and reliving some of our family's hardest and best days with me.

Jennifer Keating Hills, you have been there for me since childhood. Thank you for knowing me as Linda's daughter.

Stephanie Minor, you gave my family the gift of peace. Thank you.

Kim and Laurie Pearce, you have been like second parents to me. Rosie and Linda and Ed and Jack and Mike and Stacey live on through you.

Thank you, Grandpa Ed, for parachuting out of that plane and teaching your kids the power of faith.

To Rosie, who raised five Pearces and buried a husband and two children before their time: thank you for showing us all what it means to keep on living.

Thank you to Professor Elizabeth Taylor and the English Department at Brown University for encouraging me to write about this chapter in my family's history.

Thank you, Johanna Dobrich, for helping me learn that my past doesn't have to define my present.

To the writers who inspired me and offered their guidance during this ten-year journey: Ron Chernow, Peter Godwin, Sebastian Junger, Aidan Donnelley Rowley, and Claire Bidwell Smith—to read your books is to admire you; to talk books with you has been a dream.

Thank you to Tan Kien Huynh for opening up your home. To Mr. Bounmith for sharing your language and storied city. To Mr. Ped and Mr. Tom for helping me find that place on earth to pray. My deepest thanks to everyone I interviewed for this book: Dave Burns, Tom Combs, Rosemary Conway, Samuel Strong Dunlap, Bruce Hedlund, Dan Hensley, Carol Hrdlicka, Denise Keating, Susan Kirk, Ted Landreth, Sompatana "Tommy" Phisayavong, Robert Ramsower, Mary Simmons, Babette Smith, Cherie Stevens, Jim Spier, Adell Thompson, Richard Trencher, and Francois Vang.

Ravi, you are my rock. Thank you for bringing me a future that can draw me out of the past I've spent so many years living in.

To Mom, for being my first home, for bringing your brother home after thirty-six years, and for living and dying with such strength and grace. What I wouldn't do for one more day with you.

Ed Pearce with a photo of Jack, 1980s.

Notes

Operation Homecoming

"On prime-time news": Kim Pearce, interview with author, November 10, 2013.

He was eighteen: "Operation Homecoming for Vietnam POWs Marks 40 Years," U.S. Air Force, February 12, 2013, af.mil/News/Article-Display/Article/109716/operation-homecoming-for-vietnam-pows-marks-40-years. Accessed September 23, 2017.

My youngest uncle: Kim Pearce, interview with author, November 10, 2013.

By March 1973: Lori S. Tagg, "Operation HOMECOMING: Repatriation of American Prisoners of War in Vietnam Described," U.S. Army, December 30, 2015, army.mil/article/160491/Operation_HOMECOMING_Repatriation_of_American_prisoners_of_war_in_Vietnam_described. Accessed September 23, 2017.

Most were not: "Laos: U.S. Personnel Unaccounted for after Operation Homecoming; D.I.A. Casualty Data Summary

Included," Library of Congress, loc.gov/item/powmia/
pw159818. Accessed April 4, 2018.

a country the United States: J. Weston Phippen, "Cleaning
Up the Bombs From the Secret U.S. War in Laos," *The Atlantic,*
September 6, 2016, theatlantic.com/news/archive/2016/09/laos-
obama-bombs/498761/. Accessed January 21, 2019.

Long, thin Laos: U.S. Department of Defense, *The Pentagon
Papers: The Defense Department History of United States Decision-
making on Vietnam.* Senator Gravel Edition, sec. 1, vol. 2
(Boston: Beacon Press, 1971), 1–39.

"If Laos were": "The Pentagon Papers and United States
Involvement in Laos," in Noam Chomsky and Howard Zinn,
eds., *The Pentagon Papers.* Vol. 5, *Critical Essays* (Boston: Beacon
Press, 1972), 260.

On the day: "The Laos Crisis, 1960–1963," Office of the
Historian, history.state.gov/milestones/1961-1968/laos-crisis.
Accessed October 14, 2017.

John F. Kennedy: Sarah Kolinovsky, "The Bombing of
Laos: By the Numbers," ABC News, September 6, 2016,
abcnews.go.com/International/bombing-laos-numbers/
story?id=41890565. Accessed October 14, 2017.

Of all the: Thomas W. Lippman, "POW Pilots Left in
Laos, Files Suggest," *Washington Post,* January 2, 1994,
washingtonpost.com/archive/politics/1994/01/02/pow-
pilots-left-in-laos-files-suggest/513d8702-3edc-495e-a311-
a15040b3d465. Accessed December 9, 2019.

For years, the: Thomas W. Lippman, "U.S. Fliers Believed Held By Laos at Vietnam War's End," *Los Angeles Times*, January 2, 1994, latimes.com/archives/la-xpm-1994-01-02-mn-7768-story.html. Accessed December 9, 2019.

As my father: Charles Rotondi, interview with author, January 2, 2019.

By the end: Joshua Kurlantzick, *A Great Place to Have a War: America in Laos and the Birth of a Military CIA* (New York: Simon & Schuster, 2016), 13.

In comparison: "Vietnam War U.S. Military Fatal Casualty Statistics," National Archives, archives.gov/research/military/vietnam-war/casualty-statistics#water. Accessed January 19, 2019.

Chapter 1 / The Discovery

"I'll never give up": Andy Smith, "MIA's Sister Persists in Search for Brother," *Binghamton Press*, January 23, 1977.

"30 April 1977": Linda Pearce Rotondi, letter to President Jimmy Carter, April 30, 1977.

Chapter 2 / Gunner's Moon

Ed lies awake: My description of what happened the morning my grandparents were notified that Jack's plane was shot down are drawn from a detailed interview with them from the *Times Herald-Record* from September 3, 1980, and interviews with my uncle Kim Pearce.

Ed's B-17: Bruce Crawford, "Death on the High Road: The Schweinfurt Raid," *Aviation History*, September 1993. Available at historynet.com/world-war-ii-eighth-air-force-raid-on-schweinfurt.htm. Accessed January 22, 2019.

Ed's plane was: Edwin Pearce, letter to Veterans Administration, October 14, 1988.

Sixty-three other: Adam Claasen, *Dogfight: The Battle of Britain* (Wollombi, Australia: Exisle Publishing, 2012), 108.

Chapter 3 / Drifting

"Mothers and wives": Duke Horshock, "Families of MIA's Applaud Commando Mission," *Reading Eagle*, March 13, 1983.

Chapter 4 / Lost

"I thought it was": Elsie Kayton, "Pearce Returns from Laos Encouraged and Optimistic," *Port Jervis Union-Gazette*, October 1973.

My grandfather arrives: The detailed descriptions of Ed's itinerary and time in Laos in this chapter are drawn from his personal papers and from his interview in the *Port Jervis Union-Gazette* cited above.

Between 1964 and 1973: Erin Blakemore, "Why the U.S. Is Pledging Millions to Clean Up Bombs in Laos," *Smithsonian Magazine*, September 8, 2016, https://www.smithsonianmag.com/smart-news/why-us-pledging-millions-clean-bombs-laos-180960351/. Accessed January 21, 2019.

Or a planeload: Kolinovsky, "The Bombing of Laos."

My grandfather had: Edwin and Rosemary Pearce, interview, *Times Herald-Record*, September 3, 1980.

"It is with sincere regret": USAF colonel Carl S. Miller, letter to Edwin and Rosemary Pearce, March 29 1972.

An hour after: Edwin and Rosemary Pearce, interview, *Times Herald-Record*, September 3, 1980.

My grandfather left my: Kayton, "Pearce Returns from Laos Encouraged and Optimistic."

Ed is traveling: "MIA's Betrayed, Pearce Says," *Port Jervis Union-Gazette*, December 4, 1973.

Many had even: Air Force memo, sent to Pearce family, March 29, 1972, and Mary Simmons, interview with author, February 5, 2019.

They were all: "History of the League," National League of POW/MIA Families, pow-miafamilies.org/about-the-league.html. Accessed September 2, 2013.

Before leaving, the: "Two Fathers Leave for Laos to Learn MIA Sons' Fates," newspaper clipping, n.d.

My grandfather flew: Mary Anne McEnery, "Father Tells of Heartbreaking Search for MIAs," *Times Herald-Record*, October 26, 1973.

"I am not": Ibid.

Many of the: Bob Campbell, "Trooper Presses Mission to Find Son Lost in 1972 Combat in Laos," *Scranton Tribune*, May 1, 1975.

"Time in Laos": Kayton, "Pearce Returns from Laos Encouraged and Optimistic."

The officer startles: Ibid.

"It's something Americans": Ibid.

"It is possible": "MIA's Betrayed, Pearce Says."

"We didn't get": Lora Sharpe, "Father of MIA Soldier-Son Encouraged by Laos Visit," *Pocono Record*, October 25, 1973.

"which couldn't be refused": Kayton, "Pearce Returns from Laos Encouraged and Optimistic."

Ed waits for: Sharpe, "Father of MIA Soldier-Son Encouraged by Laos Visit."

Chapter 5 / Prometheus

"We're not looking": Jeff Gammage, "An MIA's Father Keeps the Faith," *Philadelphia Inquirer*, September 17, 1988.

Chiang Mai was: "Setthathirat I," Encyclopaedia Britannica, January 2019, britannica.com/biography/Setthathirat-I. Accessed January 30, 2019.

Roughly translated as: "Fa Ngum," Encyclopaedia Britannica, January 2019, britannica.com/biography/Fa-Ngum. Accessed January 30, 2019.

Over the centuries: Martin Stuart-Fox, *A History of Laos* (Cambridge: Cambridge University Press, 1997), 14–15.

I tell her how: Babette Smith, interview with author, January 21, 2014.

"Jack had a way": Jim Spier, interview with author, March 20, 2013.

"He wanted revenge": Kim Pearce, interview with author, November 10, 2013.

Jack's job code: Jim Spier, interview with author, March 20, 2013.

The new planes: "OV-10 Bronco Multimission Aircraft," Boeing, boeing.com/history/products/ov-10-bronco.page. Accessed February 26, 2019.

"Jack was miserable": Jim Spier, interview with author, March 20, 2013.

"The gunners on": Ibid.

"From the first": Ibid.

"Jack drank quite": Ibid.

"One night in": Ibid.

"Rarely does a": Tim Dyhouse, "Commando Hunting over Laos: Spectre Gunships in Action," *VFW Magazine*, March 2009.

"I didn't find out": Jim Spier, interview with author, March 20, 2013.

My mother had: Smith, "MIA's Sister Persists in Search for Brother."

"On the anniversary": Dave Burns, interview with author, March 29, 2013.

Chapter 6 / An American in Paris

"The Pentagon doesn't": David Launte, "Treatment of POW/ MIAs Called Stain on U.S. Honor," *Coatesville (PA) Record*, September 17, 1988.

Everything I know: All dialogue and observations from my mother's trip to Paris are from a detailed letter she wrote to my grandfather dated April 25, 1975, and a memo she wrote to the National League of POW/MIA Families describing her visits with the ambassadors. Physical descriptions are based on accompanying photographs from the trip.

Vietnam was a: Ken Burns and Lynn Novick, dirs., *The Vietnam War*, PBS, 2017.

To the French: Stuart-Fox, *A History of Laos*, 20.

France's grasp on: "Laos Profile—Timeline," BBC News, January 9, 2018, bbc.com/news/world-asia-pacific-15355605. Accessed January 30, 2019.

My mother knows: Lippman, "POW Pilots Left in Laos, Files Suggest."

"We request that": U.S. Air Force, memo sent to Pearce family, March 29, 1972.

Because America's involvement: Kurlantzick, *A Great Place to Have a War: America in Laos and the Birth of a Military CIA*, 205.

My grandparents were: "Milford Man Going to Laos in Search of Missing Son," newspaper clipping, n.d.

"All of Southeast Asia": Gene Skordinski, "Vet Claims GIs Still Alive: Government Criticized for MIA Stance," *Citizens' Voice* (Wilkes-Barre, PA), April 9, 1983.

"After explaining why": Linda Pearce Rotondi, letter to Edwin A. Pearce, April 25, 1975.

The New York Times: Richard Halloran, "Nixon and Senators at Odds on Laos Transcript," *The New York Times*, February 12, 1970, nytimes.com/1970/02/12/archives/nixon-and-senators-at-odds-on-laos-transcript.html. Accessed January 30, 2019.

And in April 1971: Kurlantzick, *A Great Place to Have a War*, 201.

"What I am": Quoted in ibid., 202.

Though more Americans: "America's Secret War in Laos," book review, *Economist,* January 21, 2017, economist.com/books-and-arts/2017/01/21/americas-secret-war-in-laos. Accessed January 30, 2019.

"Americans held no": Kurlantzick, *A Great Place to Have a War,* 205.

On April 29: Arpita Aneja and Lily Rothman, "Eyewitness to the Fall of Saigon," *Time,* April 30, 2015, time.com/3838802/fall-of-saigon-memories. Accessed January 30, 2019.

Chapter 7 / Faith

"Just as America": Richard Nixon, remarks at Armed Forces Day ceremony, Naval Station Norfolk, VA, May 19, 1973.

"I know Dad": Linda Pearce Rotondi, letter to William Jacques, April 4, 1972.

"More things are": Alice Zaengle, inscription in prayer book sent to Edwin A. Pearce while he was in Stalag 17.

Chapter 8 / Détente

"The government is": Launte, "Treatment of POW/MIAs Called Stain on U.S. Honor."

"During the Vietnam": "History of the POW/MIA Bracelets," National League of POW/MIA Families, pow-miafamilies. org/history-of-powmia-bracelets.html (accessed November 11, 2018), and "Laos: U.S. Personnel Unaccounted for after Operation Homecoming."

The previous July: Richard Nixon and L. Brezhnev, joint communiqué, Moscow, July 3, 1974. Available at washingtonpost.com/wp-srv/inatl/longterm/summit/ archive/com1974-1.htm. Accessed January 5, 2018.

"What Ed Pearce": Campbell, "Trooper Presses Mission to Find Son Lost in 1972 Combat in Laos."

"We could force": Ibid.

Then I learned: USAF major Edward E. Lindquist, Defense Clandestine Service assistant for casualty matters, "Memo for Record," January 29, 1974.

"The Vietnamese and": Richard Trencher, interview with author, February 7, 2019.

Trencher was twenty-eight: Ibid.

"The communists were": Ibid.

"When I was": Ibid.

While it now: Elizabeth Flock, "The POW/MIA Flag Still Flies High Despite Questions," *U.S. News & World Report*, February 28, 2013, usnews.com/news/articles/2013/02/28/the-powmia-flag-still-flies-high-despite-questions. Accessed February 26, 2019.

"Only those who": "Milford Man Gets First Pa. POW Plate," *Pike County Dispatch*, January 21, 1982.

"The White House": "Brooks: Ford Fears MIA Issue," *Times Herald-Record*, July 14, 1975.

1,205 American prisoners: Celestine Bohlen, "Files Said to Show Hanoi Lied in '72 on Prisoner Totals," *The New York Times*, April 12, 1993, nytimes.com/1993/04/12/world/files-said-to-show-hanoi-lied-in-72-on-prisoner-totals.html. Accessed December 9, 2019.

"The words were": "MIA's Parents Picket in D.C.," *Times Herald-Record*, November 24, 1975.

Chapter 9 / Lucky

"I want to": "Parents Hope Son's Alive in Laos," *Pocono Record*, June 1988.

"I had been": Jim Spier, interview with author, March 20, 2013.

"The Pathet Lao accused": "Laotians Charge C.I.A. 'Sabotage,'" *The New York Times*, June 14, 1975, nytimes.com/1975/06/14/archives/laotians-charge-cia-sabotage-pathet-lao-says-us-agent-tried-to.html. Accessed February 1, 2009.

"millions of dollars": Rosemary Conway, interview with author, October 13, 2013.

The June 12, 1975: American embassy in Vientiane, telegram to Henry Kissinger, June 13, 1975.

While in custody: Rosemary Conway, interview with author, October 13, 2013.

To dissuade her: Ibid.

Fortunate indeed: Nigel Cawthorne, *The Bamboo Cage: The Full Story of the American Servicemen Still Missing in Vietnam* (New York: S.P.I. Books, 1994), 278.

"The case of": American embassy in Vientiane, telegram to Henry Kissinger, June 13, 1975.

While the C.I.A.: cdn.loc.gov/master/frd/pwmia/182/57058.pdf. Accessed February 1, 2019.

One of the: Rosemary Conway, interview with author, October 13, 2013.

Conway believed Donahue: Cawthorne, *The Bamboo Cage*, 279.

In October 1987: Ibid., 281.

Chapter 10 / The Rallier

"We don't want": "Missing Serviceman's Family Has Painful Decision to Make," *Boston Herald*, November 9, 1986.

Rosemary is calling: All descriptions of events in this chapter are drawn from my grandmother's papers, especially her account entitled "How I Got Rallier's Report," which she distributed to the press and the National League of POW/MIA Families in July 1976.

"The paper has been lost": Rosemary Pearce, "How I Got Rallier's Report," July 1976.

"The paper has been destroyed": Ibid.

"If this paper": Ibid.

"How many AC-130s": Ibid.

"I would say": Ibid.

"June 8, 1977": Colonel A. W. Gratch, USAF assistant for casualty matters, letter to Linda Pearce Rotondi, June 8, 1977. Emphasis (underlined text) added by Linda Pearce Rotondi.

"The D.I.A. report": In a letter to Edwin and Rosemary Pearce dated August 4, 1976, the Air Force Personnel Center maintains that it "queried the D.I.A. on the basis of their remark that none of the crewmembers had been rescued. The response was that none had been returned to military control," giving credence to the story that the crew members were in Lao hands.

When it arrives: Edwin Pearce, letter to Congressman Joseph M. McDade, August 30, 1982.

Chapter 11 / American Imperialists

"When a country": "Milford Couple Fight U.S. for Word on Missing Son," newspaper clipping, 1983.

The Hmong were: Douglas Martin, "Gen. Vang Pao, Laotian Who Aided U.S., Dies at 81," *The New York Times*, January 8, 2011, nytimes.com/2011/01/08/world/asia/08vangpao.html?mtrref=www.google.com&gwh=E631E1860B838A2AB13B-F842B53DB16A&gwt=pay&assetType=REGIWALL. Accessed December 9, 2019.

Charismatic and prone: Kurlantzick, *A Great Place to Have a War*, 80.

But leading guerrilla: Tom Fawthrop, "Vang Pao Obituary," *The Guardian*, February 22, 2011, theguardian.com/world/2011/feb/22/vang-pao-obituary. Accessed December 9, 2019.

"Dear General Vang": Rosemary Pearce, letter to General Vang Pao, December 8, 1981.

When I ask: Francois Vang, interview with author, February 25, 2019.

Polygamy was a: Gregg Aamot, "Hmong Grapple with Effects of Polygamy," *Chippewa Herald*, November 16, 2002, chippewa.com/hmong-grapple-with-effects-of-polygamy/article_38d448fa-5fc4-5a3a-a46b-00959753b84b.html. Accessed December 9, 2019.

Vang Pao had: Fawthrop, "Vang Pao Obituary."

"What else could": Francois Vang, interview with author, February 25, 2019.

His father commanded: Martin, "Gen. Vang Pao, Laotian Who Aided U.S., Dies at 81."

"Because it was": Francois Vang, interview with author, February 25, 2019.

"Like the earth": Martin, "Gen. Vang Pao, Laotian Who Aided U.S., Dies at 81."

Who told the: Vang Pao, interview by Dr. Job L. Dittberner, Radisson Hotel, Minneapolis, MN, March 18, 1976.

Who claimed as: Ibid.

Who, in 2009: Tracie Cone, "Charges Dropped against Laotian Hero in Calif," *Newsday*, September 18, 2009, newsday.com/news/nation/charges-dropped-against-laotian-hero-in-calif-1.1459912. Accessed March 12, 2019.

"Mrs. Pearce (mother)": Captain Gary L., USAF Missing Persons Branch call log, April 16, 1973.

"[Sepon] was the": David M. Burns, *Spectre Gunner: The AC-130 Gunship* (Bloomington, IN: iUniverse, 2013), 27.

Chapter 12 / The Trial

"I had three": Status review hearing re: Senior Master Sergeant Edwin J. Pearce, board of officers convened under AFR 35-43, Randolph Air Force Base, TX, March 27, 1979.

"My husband's mother": Rosemary Pearce, letter to David Jayne, March 18, 1979.

Every word uttered: All dialogue in this chapter is excerpted verbatim from the full official transcript of the proceedings cited above.

Jack had eaten: Jim Spier, interview with author, March 20, 2013.

"'I have ended'": Ed is paraphrasing Richard Nixon's "Address to the Nation About Vietnam and Domestic Problems" from March 29, 1973.

Chapter 13 / COPE

"If the Lord": "The Secret War of Ed and Rosemary Pearce," *AM Magazine*, November 12, 1984.

American forces dropped: Kolinovsky, "The Bombing of Laos."

"A friend I": Kim Pearce, interview with author, November 10, 2013.

I have reason: Linda Pearce Rotondi, letter to President Carter, April 30, 1977.

The Pearces say: "Ten Years Later Pearces Still Look for Jack," *Pike County Dispatch*, April 8, 1982.

Chapter 14 / Politically Depressed

"34 years of": Edwin Pearce, letter to Veterans Administration adjudication officer Harry E. Roth, April 18, 1983.

"10/3/83": Peter Cupple, Mental Hygiene Clinic notes, October 3, 1983.

Ed had not: Philip M. Boffey, "Vietnam Veterans' Parade a Belated Welcome Home," *The New York Times*, November 14, 1982, nytimes.com / 1982 / 11 / 14 / us / vietnam-veterans-parade-a-belated-welcome-home.html. Accessed December 9, 2019.

"They built a": Horshock, "Families of MIA's Applaud Commando Mission."

My grandfather continues: Air Force Personnel Center, Randolph Air Force Base, unclassified Department of Defense memo to JCRC Liaison, Bangkok, Thailand, June 1984.

"Dear Mr. Bounkeut": Christine D. Miller, letter to Bounkeut Sangsomsak, chargé d'affaires ad interim, Embassy of the Lao People's Democratic Republic, July 21, 1984.

"They'd think maybe": Sompatana "Tommy" Phisayavong, interview with author, March 1, 2019.

Tommy's father was: Ibid.

Tommy's mother made: Ibid.

"5/2/85": Alan Kurlansky, Mental Hygiene Clinic notes, May 2, 1985.

His speaking tour: "The Pearces admit their search has robbed them of the ease of retirement years and the chance to devote a fair amount of attention to their other children.

But they also say they can't stop looking for their son" ("One Man's Search for a Long-Missing Son," *Pocono Record*, January 27, 1981).

"9/12/85": Alan Kurlansky, Mental Hygiene Clinic notes, September 12, 1985.

"I've seen planes": Rosa Salter, "Stymied by Red Tape and Government Intrigue, a Couple Battles to Learn the Truth About Their MIA Son," *Sunday Call-Chronicle*, November 11, 1984.

Chapter 15 / "Same-Same"

"Who is more": Edwin Pearce, op-ed, *The Journal: An Organization of Police Officers Serving Police Officers*, May 1980.

"In Seno just": Edwin Pearce, "Notes on Laos Trip," October 1973.

"Having spent most": Edwin Pearce, Journal op-ed.

Under the Lao: Georgia Catt, "A Tale of Revenge in Laos Challenges Censors," BBC News, August 26, 2012, bbc.com/news/world-asia-18770068. Accessed November 9, 2019.

Defamation is a: "Laos: Freedom of the Press," Freedom House, 2014, freedomhouse.org/report/freedom-press/2014/laos. Accessed November 9, 2019.

In 2003, two: Seth Mydans, "2 Journalists and U.S. Clergyman Are Reported Held in Laos," *The New York Times*, June 16,

2003, nytimes.com/2003/06/16/world/2-journalists-and-us-clergyman-are-reported-held-in-laos.html. Accessed November 9, 2019.

ninety thousand tons: "Sepon to Cease Gold Production," press release, MMG, November 18, 2013, mmg.com/media-release/sepon-to-cease-gold-production-d97. Accessed February 4, 2018.

Human beings have: Antonino Tucci et al., "Ancient Copper Mining in Laos: Heterarchies, Incipient States or Post-State Anarchists?" *Journal of Anthropology and Archaeology*, no. 2 (December 2014): 1–15.

Chapter 16 / White Christmas

"There's the constant": Salter, "Stymied by Red Tape and Government Intrigue, a Couple Battles to Learn the Truth About Their MIA Son."

Jack's dog tags arrive: "The ID tag pertaining to Pearce was sent registered mail (at family request) to Mr. Edwin Pearce (father) and he acknowledged receipt on 18 Dec 84" (Department of Defense Joint Chiefs of Staff message center memo, May 1985).

The sign is: Marc Schogol, "Sgt. Edwin Pearce, MIA, 3-29-72: A Couple's Memorial to a Son: Hope," *Philadelphia Inquirer*, May 25, 1986.

"Milford, PA—The": Bernard J. Collins, "Parents Told Dog Tags of Missing Flier Found," *Evening News*, March 1984.

"American Don Quixote": "Up the Gulf without a Fuel Pump, Jack Bailey, the Boat People's Friend, Is an American Don Quixote in Thailand," *People,* April 26, 1982, people.com/ archive/up-the-gulf-without-a-fuel-pump-jack-bailey-the-boat-peoples-friend-is-an-american-don-quixote-in-thailand-vol-17-no-16. Accessed December 9, 2019.

"three small packets": "PW/MIA Weekly Report," U.S. government memorandum, November 1984.

"Source, a 27": JCRC liaison office, American embassy, APO San Francisco, to JCRC commander, November 17, 1984.

In the attached: Commander Joe B. Harvey, "Refugee Report & Preliminary Evaluation," JCRC Casualty Data Division Analysis and Studies.

Chapter 17 / Just Pray

"The Pearces admit": "One Man's Search for a Long-Missing Son."

"The explosion appeared": USAF captain Howard Rowland, eyewitness report, March 30, 1972.

Chapter 18 / Archaeologists and Undertakers

"Mr. Pearce was": USAF special actions officer L. F. Scott, CWO-4, Missing Persons Branch call log, September 13, 1973.

"February 18, 1986": Peter T. White, "Missing in Action," *National Geographic*, March 1986, 692.

"At the Army's": Ibid.

"The government was": Gammage, "An MIA's Father Keeps the Faith."

"Known limited population": Ellis Kerley, report of examination, August 15, 1986.

"We had a few": Dr. Samuel Strong Dunlap, letter to Adell Thompson (brother of Robert "Skeeter" Simmons, a crew member on plane), n.d.

One anthropologist finds: Activities of the Central Identification Laboratory, hearing, Investigations Subcommittee, Committee on Armed Services, House of Representative, 99th Congress, 2nd Session, September 10, 1986, 67.

"That is more": Ibid., 69.

Dennis buried his: Ibid., 96.

Kathryn Fanning was: Ann Defrange, "MIA Wife 'Back to Square One' in Search for Spouse," *The Oklahoman*, September 22, 1985.

"She is a Marine": Rosemary Pearce, letter to Susan and Tom Kirk, August 25, 1987.

"The tags, it": Gammage, "An MIA's Father Keeps the Faith."

When the dentist: Ellis R. Kerley, letter to Mr. Nestor, March 17, 1987.

"Mrs. Pearce, we": Lieutenant Colonel Jonnie E. Webb, letter to Rosemary Pearce, October 18, 1988.

"1/15/87": Alan Kurlansky, Mental Hygiene Clinic notes, January 15, 1987.

Chapter 19 / Let Go

"They say that": Linda Pearce Rotondi, journal entry, Caring-Bridge, April 22, 2009, caringbridge.org/visit/lindarotondi/journal/view/id/51be14c26ca004253700b0de. Accessed December 11, 2013.

"a metacarpal": Joint POW/MIA Accounting Command Central Identification Laboratory, memo to Air Force Mortuary Affairs Operations, February 12, 2008.

"Chuck, when I": Linda Pearce Rotondi, Valentine's Day card to Chuck Rotondi, February 14, 2008.

"Dear Stephanie": Linda Pearce Rotondi, letter to Stephanie Minor, September 23, 2008.

Chapter 20 / The Crater

"I feel certain": Edwin and Rosemary Pearce, interview, *Times Herald-Record*, September 3, 1980.

"A former North": "D.I.A. Evaluation of Information Provided by Vietnamese Refugee," received December 4, 1990.

"I have reason": Linda Pearce Rotondi, letter to President Jimmy Carter, April 30, 1977.

About the Author

Jessica Pearce Rotondi is a writer and editor living in Brooklyn. Her work has been published by The History Channel, TIME, Reader's Digest, Salon, Atlas Obscura, HuffPost, and Refinery29. Previously, she was a senior editor at HuffPost and a staff member at the PEN American Center, the world's oldest literary human rights organization. Her first job in New York City was at St. Martin's Press, where she had a "room of her own" in the Flatiron Building to fill with books. She grew up in New England and is a graduate of Brown University. *What We Inherit* is her first book.

Connect with Jessica on Twitter and Instagram @JessicaRotondi or visit JessicaPearceRotondi.com.

■

@unnamedpress

f

facebook.com/theunnamedpress

t

unnamedpress.tumblr.com

un

www.unnamedpress.com

@unnamedpress